"Nathan is an elevator pitch expert!"
—Wall Street Journal

"Nathan delivers great insight and useful tips in this book. He covers proven strategies and techniques that will take any fear of public speaking and transform it into a valuable asset. I'm convinced readers will touch the hearts of their audiences like never before after reading this book
—Claudio Sennhauser,
Communication Skills Trainer

"Thank you, dear Nathan, for the AHA-Erlebnis. You have the power to unleash hidden capabilities in people. You truly inspired me. I had the pleasure of discovering that I was not the only one."
— Joris Vermeir, Chef and
Strategy Manager

"Nathan Gold is a black-belt pitch coach."
— Scott Case, Founding CTO Priceline.com

"I've personally benefited from Nathan's practical speaking tools and tips over the years and it is wonderful to have them put together here in Harness Your Speaking Anxiety. Nathan has a wonderful way of making what seems impossible, actually possible and even easy! Whether you have to speak to 5 or 500 people, everyone can benefit from the lessons in this practical guide."
— Scottie Spurzem, the
English Language Coach

To BJ,

Harness
Your Speaking
Anxiety

And Connect Emotionally
With Your Audience

PLEASE #PAYITFORWARD

Nathan

"I've learned that people will forget what you said, people will forget what you did, but people will never forget how you made them feel."

Maya Angelou

Harness Your Speaking Anxiety

And Connect Emotionally
With Your Audience

 **Nathan Gold**
Keynote Speaker - Presentation Coach

authorHOUSE®

AuthorHouse™
1663 Liberty Drive
Bloomington, IN 47403
www.authorhouse.com
Phone: 1 (800) 839-8640

Published by AuthorHouse 06/04/2019

ISBN: 978-1-7283-1341-2 (sc)
ISBN: 978-1-7283-1340-5 (e)

Print information available on the last page.

This book is printed on acid-free paper.

For Leigh Ann, Alaina and Felicia, my true loves.

In memory of my mother, Eleanor Sally, who taught
me what it means to live life in-service of others.

Table of Contents

PLEASE STOP HERE FIRST!

For this book to have the most impact on you, you will need occasional online access to the Internet for the complete experience. Until we have Harry Potter Live Streaming on Paper capabilities with books like this, you can find all of the content online and the videos on YouTube.

By pausing for a few minutes to listen to the music, look the photos, and watch the videos I refer to in the following chapters, you will have a similar experience as if you were sitting in my live audience. I promise the online content will make this book much more compelling for you.

HINT #1: You can use either the URL or the QR code for direct access to the content on your smartphone or tablet. If you have an iOS device, you can open your camera and simply focus on the QR code. WARNING: DO NOT SNAP A PHOTO!

You should see Safari magically pop up at the top of the screen. Click that link to take you directly to the online content.

If you use an Android device, use any QR code reader application. In either case, you can enter the URL directly in a browser on a mobile device, laptop, or desktop.

Here's an example of a QR code you can try now to see how it works on your smartphone or tablet. It should take you to www.democoach. com, which is my website.

https://www.democoach.com/

HINT #2: All of the online content you will be asked to access in this book can also all be found on one single page (password = hysa2019) accessed by the following QR code:

https://www.democoach.com/hysa

PREFACE

Hello, and thank you for choosing this book. I promise you that in these pages I will provide you with only solid nourishment and no empty calories. I will not waste your time.

Thank you for taking the time to be my audience. Thank you for allowing me to share my experiences, which are intended to help you in two areas. In Part 1 you will learn about 18 tools you can use to harness your speaking anxiety. Part 2 will then show you 10 proven ways you can connect emotionally with your audience whether an audience of one or one million.

Who will benefit from this book? Anyone who feels that speaking anxiety is hindering their potential success in business or life. It's for people who want to learn practical, proven, and simple ways to turn their biggest fear into their greatest asset. If you want to have more confidence, authenticity, and enthusiasm when you speak, this book will help you.

Why me? I've been teaching, presenting, and demoing products for over 40 years. I love this topic. I live to help people like you learn how to become more effective speakers. My career was spent in pre-sales and marketing roles for software and hardware companies such as SanDisk, Symbol Technologies, and Extensity. For the past 11 years I've been engaging with audiences around the world and preparing people for high-stakes speaking opportunities such as TED talks, keynote speeches, board meetings, investor pitches, sales presentations, and even job interviews.

The reason I wrote this book is to address the most common questions asked of me at the end of my talks and workshops. "How do I get over being nervous?" and "What do I do if I blank out during a presentation?"

My answer is usually, "There are three simple things you can easily do to manage your nerves. One, warm up your voice. Two, breathe. And three, find an energetic piece of music that you can listen to before you speak. If you blank out during a presentation, breathe, breathe, and breathe again. You should remember the next thing you wanted to talk about. Okay, any more questions? No? Have a wonderful day."

That was it! Then over the years I started to realize that fear of public speaking, or what I prefer to call speaker anxiety, is more severe for people than I thought. I often feel anxiety when I speak, and I give at least 100 talks every year. So I wrote this book to help all you who want to learn how to speak more effectively, especially when it involves something you genuinely believe and care about.

There is one caveat. Every tool I share assumes that you are already prepared with your content. This includes any media such as slides, videos, pictures, devices, sensors, 3D printed models, and other items you show your audience. I am also assuming that you have prepared by rehearsing your talk or presentation many times out loud by yourself or in front of "real" people.

PART 1:
INTRODUCTION

So why are you holding this book in your hands? Why are you interested in harnessing your speaking anxiety? There's a straightforward answer. It's because we all have a fear of speaking in public. Glossophobia is a social fear of public speaking and it affects everyone.

For the remainder of this book I will refer to glossophobia as "speaking anxiety" to keep things simple. Everybody experiences it to some degree. You probably would admit that you have some form of uncontrolled or possibly controlled nervousness or what I call speaking anxiety. The challenge is to make sure that it doesn't get in the way of your success. My guess is that if I could sit down with you for 10-15 minutes I would quickly find that speaking anxiety IS getting in the way of some part of your potential success.

Perhaps you even have speaking anxiety when you have an idea to share in a meeting. Surrounded by a group of executives, you perhaps tell yourself, "Nah. I won't say anything this time. It's a dumb idea anyway."

However, the idea you have in mind could be what flips the whole direction of your project or company. And just like that you're all having a much better time and greater success because you dared to speak up. The occasion may also be a job interview or a formal address to a thousand people. These are all anxiety-inducing situations. Whenever an emcee introduces me, I always feel the same anxiety or butterflies that other people feel. The difference is that my butterflies are flying in formation. You'll understand why later.

Let's make sure that your speaking anxiety is not impeding your success anymore. It's time to turn one of your biggest fears into your most significant asset by using the tools, techniques, and tips you will learn in this book.

Isn't the black stallion in this picture a majestic and powerful looking animal? Let that image burn into your mind. Why? Because from this moment forward whenever you feel butterflies, whenever you feel speaking anxiety, I want you to imagine that black stallion. Metaphorically speaking, the black stallion is your speaking anxiety. Think of it as what soon will be your most trusted companion.

All you need to do, using the tools provided in this book, is to harness the energy you feel before you open your mouth to speak in public. It's much like harnessing a horse to get the animal to do what you want it to do. Of course, as with any skill, it takes practice.

One more thing. During the weeks leading up to a presentation, speaking anxiety is rarely experienced the way it will be on the appointed day. It is crucial that you take small steps forward before the actual speaking day.

Most people tell me that they most frequently feel speaking anxiety mostly during the few minutes before they have to talk and then for the first 30 or so seconds. Once they get through those 30 seconds, they are usually fine. So what we are talking about here is how to harness your speaking anxiety in those few minutes and seconds. That's it!

DISCLAIMER: I am not a medical doctor. I can't help you with debilitating anxiety, the type of fear that keeps you from leaving your house and may require medical attention. But I want it to be clear that I have helped thousands of people over the last decade harness their speaking anxiety. Know that all of the tools in this book work in many different situations.

I am confident when I say that you can't "get over" nervousness or speaking anxiety. You merely need to learn how to harness it the way you harness a horse to get it to work for you or go in the direction you want it to take you.

I've helped TED and TEDx speakers prepare for their time on stage. If you want to experience extreme speaking anxiety, try walking into a room with Bill Gates, Warren Buffett, and Al Gore sitting in the front row. That's an anxiety-causing situation for sure! Without using some of the tools in this book, your chances of making an excellent presentation in such a scenario are slim.

Back when I was growing up, Batman was my favorite TV hero. Why? Because I wanted a girlfriend like Batgirl. No, I'm kidding.

It was really because of the bat belt—the utility toolbelt. As a child I thought, "I want to wear one of those belts for my whole life. That way, any situation in which I find myself, I can pull out the tool I need and save myself, my family, and my friends."

So, what I'm going to do for you in this book is to give you a metaphorical toolbelt in the form of practical ideas you can start implementing right away. It's going to be quick and straightforward, just as some of the best things in life are.

Let's get started.

Here are three examples of people with different degrees of speaking anxiety to illustrate how it affects every one of us.

I had a client many years ago named Peter. He was 45 years old at the time and suffered from tremendous speaking anxiety. Why? Because when he was nine and on stage as the main character in his school play, he froze. The teacher had to whisper all his lines from behind a curtain. He suffered the humiliation and embarrassment of standing there for five minutes. That experience carried through the rest of his life until I met him 36 years later. Peter avoided every speaking opportunity in his career because of that one situation.

Have any of you experienced that sort of traumatic situation? If so, it's time to harness your speaking anxiety and move on.

How about Ringo Starr of the Beatles? He has admitted to anxiety every time he has to go on stage. A few seconds before his entrance, he usually felt like running away. The way he dealt with it was by running up on stage. By the time he got to his place behind the drums, his anxiety had subsided, and he was fine.

Sometimes doing something as simple as running to your mark on stage or coming in from the back of the room instead of the front can reduce your speaking anxiety. Usually, I'm told, "Just as soon as I get over those first 30 seconds, I'm fine." So it's a very short period of time about which we're worried.

Finally, I'll use myself as an example of someone who experiences speaking anxiety. That's right. Even I experience speaking anxiety. However, most of the time it's an excited can't-wait-to-share-with-you speaking anxiety, which keeps me on my toes and allows me to engage my audiences for many hours at a time.

Seven years ago I was thrown into the most stressful anxiety-causing situation I have ever experienced. It was wholly unexpected and temporarily threw me off my game.

I had been asked by the Kauffman Foundation in Kansas City, Missouri, to record a video series on "Powerful Presentations." I hopped on a plane, got to the hotel, and enjoyed a decent sleep. In the morning I was whisked off to the Kansas City Performing Arts Center where the filming was scheduled to be done. I was expecting a small side room, two people, and one camera.

However, when I walked into the main hall where the filming was taking place, I almost had a heart attack. Why? There were nearly 20 people from a local television filming crew with two cameras on rolling tracks, lights, mics, and even a makeup artist for me to look my best in every shot. It was not like anything I had experienced in my life until then.

I had to ask Sharon, my makeup artist, to get me away from the situation for a few minutes to calm myself down. I was sweating profusely, and the lights weren't even on yet. The light blue shirt I was wearing was already drenched. It was a good thing that I had been told to bring several shirts for the shoot.

The main point I want to make here is that no matter how experienced you are at presenting your ideas, products, or services, we all feel speaking anxiety to different degrees based on the situation and people involved. In the situation I've just described, I had to use several of the tools I'm going to share with you in this book to get back to my senses before they could start filming.

How we harness that anxiety and turn it into an asset is what this book is all about.

Check out "Michael Bay, Samsung CES 2014":

http://bit.ly/2ILxq3x

That was the Samsung announcement of the first curved television at CES 2014 in front of thousands of people and now millions more on YouTube. Don't you think that might be one of the most uncomfortable situations that a man has ever found himself faced with?

Michael Bay is the third highest revenue-grossing movie producer in Hollywood. Did you catch it? There was a teleprompter in front of him, but something went wrong. Bay had no Plan B. Things went from bad to worse until he walked off the stage.

No Plan B? You would think somebody like Bay could talk to any audience. Even the emcee tried to help him by saying, "Tell us about the curve and how it will affect your movies."

That's why Bay was there, by the way, to talk about the new curved TV when Samsung was first introducing it. Bay couldn't even get his senses together enough to speak an intelligent sentence.

So why did that happen to him, and why can it happen to you, me, or any of us? There's one main reason. Part of our brain called the amygdala signals the fight-or-flight response. It's the "I'm going to protect you at all costs if you get into a dangerous situation" response that operates without the need for thinking or logical decision-making.

His amygdala kicked in, and Michael Bay wanted out. He could not think straight because, when the amygdala activates, rationality in the neocortex temporarily disconnects. It's not required to decide to fight or run when danger is present. Bay was unable to think, and he did not know what to do except leave the stage. That was the flight response in action.

If cave dwellers sat around thinking, "I've got five hungry lions coming at me right now. Should I go home to my family, or should I stay and fight? I don't know. What do you think, Joe?" they would be food for the wild animals. Even though we are not usually in danger of being eaten, we still feel the fight-or-flight response.

Speaking anxiety afflicts each of us in varying degrees. I have tremendous anxiety when I speak to groups of 30 or more. One of the reasons I'm thinner than I probably ought to be is that my fourth-grade teacher said, "You're going to be thin your whole life because you worry too much." So it's true. I worry.

I have speaking anxiety just like any other healthy person. However, mine is in what I refer to as the "Blue Zone" where it is more about the joy, excitement, and childlike anticipation of meeting a group of new people and sharing my information with them. On the other side of the spectrum is what I call the "Red Zone" where it is about fear, uncertainty, and doubt. Most people are somewhere in the middle when they speak. This book will give you tools you can use to get yourself into the Blue Zone.

EXPERIMENT: Let's try a simple experiment to get started. Are you ready?

All right. I want you to start a 60-second countdown timer. At the end of the 60 seconds I'm going to ask you to call me on the telephone to deliver a one-minute presentation about a time in your life when you failed at something. Okay? Stay with me.

Tick-tock. Tick-tock. Tick-tock. Are you thinking about what story you will use or perhaps starting to feel a bit of speaking anxiety?

Tick-tock. Tick-tock. Tick-tock. Time is up. It's time to pick up the phone right now and call me to share that story. Okay? No. Not for real. However, I was trying to get you to feel some speaking anxiety right now before we got too much further.

See how easy it can be to feel anxiety?

If I asked you how that speaking anxiety manifested itself, these are some of the things you would tell me:

- ✓ Pounding/racing heart
- ✓ Tunnel vision
- ✓ Neck and shoulder tension
- ✓ Butterflies in your stomach

- ✓ Shortness of breath
- ✓ Cold, clammy hands
- ✓ A blank mind
- ✓ Dry mouth
- ✓ Sweaty palms and armpits

Speaking anxiety manifests itself in each of us in varying degrees based on the specific situation. Perhaps your stomach tightened up. Maybe you started breathing a little more shallowly. Probably your heart rate increased. Perhaps you started perspiring a bit. Maybe you started thinking, "I'd better figure out quickly what I am going to talk about!"

If you did not feel any speaking anxiety just now, it's okay. However, I know that in the past you have felt it perhaps hundreds of times, which is one reason why you are holding this book now.

Let's take that feeling and put a harness on it so that you can start benefiting from it. It's time to turn one of your biggest fears into one of your most significant assets.

To get started, you need to follow three steps. Step 1 is to acknowledge that you have speaking anxiety. It's normal. That black stallion is inside you. It represents your speaking anxiety. In fact you've already taken Step 1 since you are reading these words right now. You've already acknowledged that you are challenged by speaking anxiety.

Step 2 is to ask yourself, "What's the worst thing that could happen if I speak up in a meeting or go up on stage and speak for an hour?" When you consider the worst that could happen, it's not that bad after all. When things go wrong when you speak, and they sometimes do, it's okay. An audience usually understands when things don't go perfectly. It makes you human, approachable, more like your audience. No speaker or presentation is ever perfect. Why strive for perfection anyway? Aiming for excellence is much more fun, and when you achieve it you usually feel it in your bones.

Step 3 is to ease into the mindset. Remember that everyone has some form or degree of speaking anxiety. It's a matter of to what degree you have it and in which situations. If you're going to deliver a TED talk, it's a very different level of anxiety than if you're making a presentation to executives at your office, your peers, or even your friends and family. It's an even different situation when you meet a new customer alone. Let's start figuring out how to harness your speaking anxiety.

One way to get over your fear of public speaking is to attack it with a vengeance. If you let it control you for the rest of your life, you'll miss out on opportunities you can only dream of. It's possible that you may be getting in the way of success by not talking to yourself in more positive terms especially before you speak.

It is helpful if you imagine a more favorable outcome and engage in positive dialogue with yourself. Try using the language you would use with someone you love. It might be a little different from what you are telling yourself right now.

And, yes, that might be a bit of a fake-out for your mind. However, what's the alternative? Imagining a terrible outcome? Try adding a positive attitude to what you're doing when you speak. One of the biggest reasons why people become better speakers is that they have a positive attitude toward themselves and their audience.

1: BREATHE

Let's try a simple one-minute exercise. Ready? Please get comfortable in a sitting position. Sit upright with your shoulders back. Then breathe in deeply, hold it for a few seconds, and breathe out slowly while telling yourself to relax. You can say this silently or out loud, depending on who is nearby.

Okay? Please repeat this drill a couple more times. Wasn't that easy? How do you feel right now?

Breathing is the number-one tool and most important thing you can do when you experience speaking anxiety. If you take nothing else away from this book, remember to remind yourself to breathe deeply and more often.

I can tell what you might be thinking. "Wait a minute, Nathan. That is ridiculous. I'm already breathing." Yes, you're breathing, but you are not breathing sufficiently for what you are about to do. Typically, you're not taking in enough air for your body and brain to function correctly when you are feeling speaking anxiety.

When you get stressed or nervous about addressing a group of people, your breathing rate usually shortens. You take very shallow breaths high in the lungs, and your body is not getting enough oxygen.

After that deep-breathing exercise I had you do a few minutes ago, do you feel more relaxed? You should. If not, try it again.

Remember, controlled breathing is *the* essential tool for harnessing speaking anxiety. You will always need to remind yourself to breathe correctly depending on the intensity of your anxiety.

Let's explore another reason why you might not be breathing correctly in Chapter 2.

2: POSTURE

Good posture allows you to breathe deeply and more easily. If your posture is terrible or you slouch, your lungs can't do what they need to do! One reason you might be feeling you are in the Red Zone of speaking anxiety is because you are just not standing tall.

Before I step in front of people or am being introduced to an audience, I push my arms back, expand my chest, and breathe deeply so that my posture will help me to feel more confident.

I'm a pretty confident person, but if you saw me standing in line and waiting for a bus I tend to slouch. I admit it: I'm lazy when it comes to my posture.

However, when I walk up on stage in front of people, I stand so that I look taller and occupy more space. Doing so makes me automatically feel more confident. And not only will you feel more confident, but your audience will also think you're more confident. So check your posture when you speak to see if it needs adjustment.

There are several ways to improve your posture. I'm not here to tell you what to do to improve your posture. Just get somebody to take a side-shot photo of you standing or a video of you walking. Then you can see for yourself.

If your posture is right and you like how you look, move on. If it's not, then maybe explore some things you can do about it such as improv. I suggest you go to an improv meet-up in your area. They teach you in an enjoyable and safe environment that the most straightforward way you can look more substantial in a room is to use your posture and gestures. and hands. You want to stand tall, walk tall. When you do that, you will enhance your presence in any room, not just the ones with a stage.

3: FIND YOUR VOICE

It might sound strange for someone like me to tell you that you can harness your speaking anxiety by finding your voice. The key word is "your," meaning that the *normal* tone and volume of your voice might not be the best register to use when you are trying to persuade someone or a group of people to take action. You may need to find a voice that allows you to transfer your enthusiasm for what you are talking about to your audience.

Your normal voice may not achieve this goal unless you are lucky enough to have a "radio voice," the kind you can listen to for long periods of time without getting distracted. You've undoubtedly heard people say that it's not what you say but how you say it. I believe that it's a lot about how you say it.

In most of my talks and workshops I love to illustrate how voice should not be taken for granted or as an afterthought. Your voice is the most powerful tool you have when you speak in public! Finding the voice inside you that allows you to speak with more authority, confidence, poise, eloquence, power, emphasis, and even persuasiveness may not be coming from your ordinary normal everyday voice.

Here's an exercise I run during my workshops to prove to people that there's more to their voice than they think. I ask everyone to think of a short story they will share with the group. I usually ask them to tell the story in under a minute. It can be either a true or invented story. However, there is a caveat.

The person telling the story is allowed to use only one word for the entire story. The word is "blah." You should see faces in the audience when I ask participants to do this. Since most of them have never been asked to do this, I always demonstrate how it sounds: "Blah (waving to one person). Blah (waving to another person). Blah blah blah (pointing to my watch). Blah blah blah blah blah blah blah (indicating I was sleeping). Blah blah blah! (waking up suddenly as if I missed the alarm). Blah blah blah."

During this demonstration people often laugh or chuckle because without real words I must use other techniques to engage and communicate with my audience.

When I take your words away, which is the one thing that speakers spend most of their time preparing, you automatically have to rely on two things that often get overlooked. Those are how your voice sounds (volume, pacing, tone, pitch, emphasis, and even pauses) and what you do with your body (posture, use of arms and hands, facial expressions, and manipulation of space).

Remember that whenever you speak your words are only one part of the message your listeners receive. Please remind yourself that your voice and body language are a significant part of speaking and how people process what you say to them.

Another reason why I wanted to share this exercise is that you may need to find your speaking or oratorical voice—the voice that when you talk makes auditors consider you persuasive, compelling, and memorable. It's a little bit of an act until you find that authentic voice you are comfortable using anywhere.

My voice when I am presenting is not my usual one. I vary its tone, pitch, and cadence to be sure that I am engaging my listeners at every point during my presentations and workshops. If you and I were at a table right now, I would not be talking with the same level of enthusiasm I use on stage because you would not want to be sitting with me. I might use gestures, but I'm not going to speak in the loud voice I use to get to the back of the room in a public venue.

You'll find that a big way to reveal your enthusiasm is by how you sound. Let your heart speak through your voice. That way, believe me, you'll sound more compelling, honest, and authentic.

4: CREDIBILITY

Establishing your credibility for listeners is a major tool in harnessing speaking anxiety. Once your audience respects and trusts you, it's much easier to have an impact on people. If the individual who introduces you to an audience does not establish your credibility in advance, it's up to you to do so.

During my time as a speaking coach I found that most people are unwilling to talk about themselves even when they need to establish their credibility for an audience. Some are even unwilling to reveal that they have an advanced degree in a subject relevant to the subject of the presentation!

I am not suggesting that you brag about yourself. However, it is crucial that you are able to validate yourself in a few sentences. I am not talking about reading your résumé or Curriculum Vitae to an audience.

What I like to refer to as a "humble brag" establishes your credibility with an audience. It can be as simple as saying, "Ten years ago when I was completing my Ph.D. my team, and I discovered . . ." or "After talking with 80% of our customers face-to-face, I can share some things with you that will likely be surprising, but they are absolutely true and offer insight into our next product offering."

You don't have to elaborate at length on your education or success to date. When you indicate that you have a Ph.D. on your title slide or mention the fact in your opening, people generally respond very positively. Those three letters or some other advanced degree or a recognizable certification warrants your credibility for most audiences.

I can hear what you're thinking right now: "I don't have a Ph.D. or Master's or certification." I get it. Neither do I! That is when you need to reflect on what you have done and single out one thing that establishes your credibility.

Establishing one's credibility can be compared to how four legs balance a table. The first leg is having expertise or specialization in something. That's a given. Whether this leg includes an advanced degree is not essential. What's important is that whatever you tell people leads them to believe you know what you're talking about.

Now, do you believe or trust every expert you meet? Most people say, "Heck no." That's the second leg. Build trustworthiness into every aspect of how you conduct yourself. Everything about you needs to project the impression that this is a trustworthy person.

The third leg of credibility is that you need to care. Whether you're trying to convince an investor to subsidize your venture or trying to get a customer to use your prototype, you need to show that you are doing it for the right reasons.

In essence, you need to show that you want to be of service to others. When you show that you care about what you are doing AND your audience, people will want to do more business with you. They will act based on what you share with them.

One of my favorite quotations will help you reframe your thinking in this regard. It comes from a good friend of mine named John K. Bates. As a TED coach he tells people, "Make the audience the hero in your talk, not you."

This advice should make you think about your audiences. With this outlook you automatically start wanting to be more helpful. You have to care because you're in it for your audience. That's what differentiates great speakers from average speakers. The ones who are caring want to help you. They genuinely want you to walk out with more than you came in with.

There's still one more leg to balance out the metaphorical table of credibility. The fourth leg is the one that most people give up on, forget, or hold back. It's called enthusiasm.

When many people speak in front of others, quite often their enthusiasm drops through the floor, or they leave it at home. Maybe they don't want others to know how excited they are about their subject. I don't know why. There are probably 1,001 reasons why. When enthusiasm is not a significant part of your presentation, however, you're missing out on being memorable. Listeners will not forget you if you project honest and genuine enthusiasm. They will talk about you and share with others what they heard you say.

When you combine the other three aspects of credibility with enthusiasm, your effectiveness as a speaker skyrockets. Your effectiveness gets even stronger as you continue working on it. Moreover, the more you care and the more you want to help and the more you build your trustworthiness, believe it or not the less your expertise or credentials matter.

5: WHAT ARE YOU WORKING ON?

In general, people are interested in what you are working on. You have probably heard the question, "What are you working on?" thousands of times in your life. Perhaps the question will be phrased as "What does your company do?" or "What does your product do?" or "What do you do for a living?" Such inquiries are incredible opportunities to connect emotionally with people by giving a compelling answer.

I wager, every one of you reading this book has often been asked this question. Whether you work for a big company, small firm, government agency, nonprofit company, academic institution, or a startup, people will ask what you do or what you do for a living. If you are a recent graduate looking for a job or perhaps advancing your career in a new direction, people will ask, "What do you want to do?" or "What kind of company do you want to work for?"

The typical answer to such questions, however, goes something like this: "We make a wearable sensor that tracks your sun exposure. Yada. Yada. Yada." The yada's are more soundbites about the features of the product or service.

Very often all you need to do to add impact to this answer is to spin it slightly. For example, "We make a wearable sensor that tracks your sun exposure to let you know when you need more or when you have had enough." Do you hear the difference in this answer as compared to the first one? People need to understand the value and benefits they receive in order to become interested in your product or service.

There's one more crucial aspect of your response. It's not only about giving a clear, compelling, and memorable answer. It's also important to consider whether a person or audience can repeat what they heard you say or paraphrase it. Word of mouth is still one of the most powerful forms of dissemination. When you give people a compelling answer, and they can repeat it, you are on your way to more success.

If you can be literal in your answer and elicit a visceral response from your audience, go for it. Be straight up in your answer if you have the cure for cancer or anything that powerful. "We have discovered the cure for cancer." That's enough for people to respond by saying something like, "Whoa! I want to know more." They will lean forward. They will be curious.

Most of the time when you tell people what you are working on, though, it's a little more ordinary. So let's see what you can do to tweak your answer to get people intrigued and reduce your speaking anxiety at the same time.

Here are two vivid examples to illustrate this point:

There's a wild ride you can take on the Zero-G airplane that lets you experience weightlessness without going into space. It's not 100% zero gravity because you must go into space for that. What people experience on this airplane is called microgravity. It looks like great fun from the pictures of people up there.

What do you think microgravity feels like? It feels like something physical we've all done here on Earth.

Usually, when I ask this question in my workshops, somebody responds by saying swimming or floating in water. That's exactly what it feels like according to two people I have met who have experienced the phenomenon. So if I'm a Ph.D. specializing in microgravity and walk into a room to speak about the topic, how many in an audience even care about microgravity if all they want to do is to go up in that plane?

If I bored you to tears with what microgravity is and how it affects your organs, you'd doze off, and my speaking anxiety would increase. One way to reduce your anxiety and increase interest in your topic is to make it so simple for listeners that they cannot possibly forget the presentation.

Rather than launching into a technical discussion, all I have to do is start by saying something like, "Microgravity is just like floating in a pool," and everybody gets it. Now you can move on. You don't need the preliminary detail. Of course, you would not do this if your audience were scientists and researchers because it might be taken as insulting. I know that's a ridiculously simple example, but stay with me.

Here's the second and powerful example of how one presenter made everyone laugh or smile and look up:

I once saw a presenter jump up on stage and do something incredible. There were several presenters before him, and they had all been fairly boring. So this guy gets up on stage and starts with these exact words: "Ladies and gentlemen, I'm thrilled to be here to share with you the machines we build that turn water into money."

When he said this, almost 300 of us in the audience started smiling, laughing, looking up, and wondering what this guy's product was all about. He certainly caught our attention. We thought, "Yeah, right. Come on. Show us!"

Then he projects a picture of a small canal turbine. "This is what we build," he says. "It's about a meter wide under those yellow housings are microturbines. You throw this into any rushing waterway, tie it off to the side, and plug it in. As soon as those flappers start spinning, you're generating free electricity."

I am confident that the audience would *not* have reacted in the same way if he had started with something literal such as saying, "We build canal turbines." This would not have made us laugh or look up.

You need to think about getting your listeners curious. Get them leaning forward. Get them wanting to know more. That's what 30-second commercials do on TV, don't they? They don't tell you everything about everything. They get you to take action, which is what most speakers are trying to do with their listeners.

Enough examples. Here are things you can do to amp up your answer to the question, "What are you working on?"

First, you can be literal by using a value-proposition formula such as Steve Blank's "We help X do Y by doing Z," where X is whom you help, Y is what you do for them, and Z is how you do it. You don't have to use all the parts of this formula. It all depends on what you are trying to do with your audience and who they are.

"We put people on the moon." "We discovered the cure for cancer." Those are literal answers. "We make a sensor that passes vibration data from any machine on the planet to yada, yada, yada."

If your answer like the last one is boring, you need to think about the words you are using. Maybe a good simile, analogy, or metaphor is all you need to help your audience follow you more effectively and become interested. We communicate by using similes, analogies, and metaphors all of the time, so why not use them in a presentation? Most people respond to such statements as "Microgravity is like swimming" or "We build a machine that turns water into money" with curiosity. Now that's a good start!

6: MEET AND GREET

One of my favorite tools for reducing anxiety about speaking engagements and presentations is to Meet and Greet the people who come into a room early. I try to talk to at least 8-10 people before the event so I get some general idea of who they are and what they expect. Knowing a few people in your audience before you start speaking can instantly lower whatever anxiety you may have.

You also might be able to refer to those people during your talk or perhaps ask them a question you know they can answer. You might even start your talk by referring to some of the people you met. For example, "I was talking to Kai, Jean, John, Alice, and Jane earlier. All of you told me that you hope this talk will help you get a handle on [fill in the blank]. I promise it will. Let's get started."

My favorite questions to ask people attending my presentations are "Why did you come here?" and "What do you hope to get out this talk?" I always want to be sure people are in my audience for the right reasons. Otherwise I may need to adjust my talk on the spot.

As an extreme example, I once had a two-hour workshop with MBA students from overseas planned out when I left my office that morning. After I arrived at the talk's location, the organizer told me that there had been a common theme in questions the students asked all of the presenters during the prior week. When she enumerated the questions, I realized that my talk was going to answer none of them.

Making a quick adjustment, I therefore opened as follows: "Ladies and gentlemen, thank you for your time today. I want to be sure that we don't waste even a minute of our two-hour workshop together.

So, rather than use high-tech slides, I'm going old-school with a whiteboard talk today. My understanding from the organizer is that you have five main questions on your minds today. How about we start with those questions and see if there is any time left at the end. Okay? Great! Let's go. Topic one is time."

The response was overwhelmingly positive. The organizer afterwards told me that the students were so appreciative of my not wasting their time and answering the most important questions they had on their minds. My talk was the one they kept referring back to over the final week of their program. When you do not waste people's time and over-deliver value, you stand out as a speaker for all the right reasons.

This would not have happened if I had assumed that my original content was going to work. I was open to change, and you need to be too. The key is, it is all about your audience, not you.

7: WARM-UP ROUTINE

A warm-up routine is an essential tool for harnessing your speaking anxiety. Warming up is not reserved for sports. A good warm-up routine is a part of being an accomplished speaker just as in any situation where you need to perform such as acting or singing.

Sports analogies are overused in presentations and books, but this one is appropriate. I was at UC Berkeley waiting for a meeting one day with an hour to kill, so I walked into the football stadium where the team was warming up a few hours before an upcoming game.

While sitting in the stands, I was mesmerized by the center, the guy who hikes the ball to the quarterback. He was off by himself toward the side of the field with no one around him. He was going through his routine up to the point where he would hike the ball and then stop before walking a few steps away. Then he'd walk back to the same spot and do it again. It was like a perfectly choreographed dance in which every move was calculated and repeated, even the number of steps he walked. It was amazing to watch.

Do you need that kind of warm-up routine before you speak? It depends. Maybe for a TED talk. If you're presenting to your peers, perhaps all you need to do is to walk faster to the front of the room that day and high-five people along the way to generate some energy in the room. Then you might feel less anxiety when you get to the front.

Each of you needs to form your own warm-up routine. No routine will work for everyone in all situations. I could share what my warm-up routine is, but it's not that important. Just make up your own and always start with controlled breathing.

When I was watching that football player at UC Berkeley, he took three deep breaths before the next part of his warm-up routine. It was precisely three breaths every time, and he did this no fewer than 25 times while I sat there. It was an incredibly instructive lesson.

8: THE FIRST-30

People often tell me, "If I can just get through the first 30-seconds, I'll be fine." I understand that most people consider the first half-minute the most important part of a presentation because it sets the tone for the rest of your delivery. If you have prepared your information, slides, stories, demoware, questions, and props and if you have rehearsed your talk numerous times, there are easy ways to manage your first 30-seconds without getting into the talk itself.

Here are a few tricks you can use that work in just about any situation. You start by incorporating the first two tools we've already covered earlier. Ready?

First, as you consciously remind yourself to breathe more deeply than usual, walk up in front of your audience and give them a genuine, honest, and authentic smile. Pause for a moment and look around the room. That's a beautiful way to start. You'll even feel better when you smile.

Second, make sure you stand tall with the best posture you can muster. You can slouch later on, but in the first 30-seconds stand as tall as you can. Meanwhile continue to breathe deeply.

Third, in an enthusiastic voice say, "Good morning." You can easily remember that as your first line, right? If it's the afternoon or evening, adjust accordingly. If you say, "Good morning and welcome to [fill in the blank]" and it's the evening, nobody cares anyway. If it's the evening and you say, "Good morning," people will good-naturedly smile, chuckle, or laugh. And that's good too.

At this point you're about five seconds into your time and need more to say that will help with the initial speaking anxiety. I have just the thing for most situations.

It's been my experience that one of the most critical points a speaker needs to make at the beginning of a presentation is how much time he or she will be talking. I know this may sound strange. But I also know from 40+ years of starting with this gambit that people appreciate your showing respect for their time right up front.

The next thing you can say is something like, "In the next two hours . . ." or "I have you for two hours, and in that time I. . . ." When you start this way, your listeners will most likely think to themselves, "Okay. Two hours. I got it. I'm here for two hours." The audience will also feel better about you because you value their time.

There are many ways you can cover this step this before you get to the topic at hand. You can say something to this effect: "Good morning, ladies and gentlemen. In the next 25-minutes that I have with you here today, I plan to . . . Are there any questions before we start?" You've just taken 30-seconds. By now you should be more in control of your speaking anxiety. You may even have forgotten about it because you did something a little different than most speakers, and your audience will be looking forward to what you have to say.

After the first 30-seconds you can easily segue to "Okay, let's get started" and then get to your content. By this time your speaking anxiety should be right where you want it to be—calm but excited and enthusiastic.

9: WHAT IF?

The next question generally on the minds of people at this point is, "Okay. That's great for the first 30 seconds, but what if I blank out or get stuck in the middle of the presentation? What if I can't remember what comes next?"

This happens to all speakers, myself included. Let me share an experience I had recently. I have been talking about speaking anxiety and the simplest three things that people can do to manage it for years. A while ago I was 16 hours ahead of myself in Dubai when I said, "Here are the three things you can do to manage your nervousness before you speak. One is to do this, and two. . . . I'll get back to that. Three is to do this." I gave them the third one without covering the second. I had said these lines so many times before. The speech was in there, but I just had to let it come out of my jet-lagged brain.

So what's happening at such moments is that your amygdala is doing its job, "Bye-bye thinking brain. I don't need you." At times like this, you can't find what you can't remember no matter how hard you look. You need to get your senses back and quickly. The way to do so is by using one or more of the following techniques.

1. Take a few slow, calming breaths. You were probably not breathing very well when you locked up. Relax and let your brain think while you breathe. The pause will give you time to think, and it will allow the audience to reflect on what you have said so far. A longish pause can have a positive impact on your audience, especially if it happens at the right moment.

2. Mindmapping is a very effective way to chart your entire talk on a single sheet of paper that can be with you on stage if you need it. The technique was invented by Tony Buzan, and it's my favorite way to make sure that you don't get lost in the middle of a presentation. See Chapter 11 for more details.

3. You can also use a simple list or outline written on a small index card. Referring to it will connect your thinking brain back to your feeling brain.

4. Move to another location if possible. The physical movement might be just what you need to jog your memory. Get some water if you have to and drink some. No one will ever fault you for sipping some water. Whatever you do, *don't* say, "I can't remember what's next, folks." That's just an excuse. Don't make up excuses for your audience to feel sympathetic toward you. It usually backfires. Most audiences don't like excuses. So get some water and come back. You should be okay because you should be breathing better after moving and drinking.

5. If you tried the preceding four techniques and still don't know what to say next, just go on to the next topic. So what that you forgot to talk about one thing. Your audience may ask a question about it later. Big deal! If you forget something important during your presentation, hopefully somebody will ask a question to which you can respond, "Oh, yes, that's right. I forgot to address that when I was talking about. . . ." This type of situation makes you more human in the minds of your listeners. Just roll with it. Stuff you don't necessarily plan on happens all the time.

6. As a last resort, if you think it will not sound like an excuse, be honest with your audience. Caring and open speakers tend to be likable. Don't try to fake your way out of it or even make jokes. If you

lock up, you lock up. It generally won't happen so severely that you can't compensate, unlike Michael Bay who was in front of thousands of people when he walked off the stage.

The bottom line is that when you are prepared you need to trust in yourself.

10: REVERSE SPEAKING ANXIETY

Parenthetically to all of the preceding chapters and guidelines, I want to make you aware of something most people have never heard of. This is a phenomenon I call reverse speaking anxiety. It signifies a situation in which a speaker inadvertently causes anxiety for listeners, which in turn causes more anxiety for the speaker.

The first way to cause anxiety for your audience is by starting late. Sometimes a late start is unavoidable owing to factors beyond a speaker's control, but even under those circumstances a delay can be managed effectively. As soon as the scheduled start time gets within a minute, walk up to the front of the room and say something like, "Ladies and gentlemen, I want to thank you for arriving on time or even early. I've been asked to wait a few more minutes to get started. So you are the lucky ones who have time to get a refill on your coffee or tea. You've got the best seats in the house, and we'll get started in ten more minutes. Thank you again."

If those in the audience are like me, they likely will be thinking, "Okay, good. Now I can get more coffee and meet some new people."

A second way in which speakers can cause reverse anxiety is by saying, "Raise your hand if. . . ." A listener is probably thinking, "What? Do I have to raise my hand? What if they call on me and I have to speak in front of all of these people?"

A third way in which speakers cause anxiety for listeners occurs when they do what many presentations-skills books suggest as an ice-breaker: "I'd like to ask you a question. Who here has had an experience in which . . .?" If an audience member hears that pitch, what is he or she probably thinking? "Uh oh. What if they call on me? If I raise my hand, I have to talk in public. Forget it."

Be kinder to and less manipulative of your audiences. Make sure that they know you're the kind of speaker who is going to be helpful to them, and then you can ask them all sorts of questions. Don't cause speaking anxiety in your audience, especially at the beginning of your talk.

11: MINDMAPPING

If you want to harness your speaking anxiety by helping your brain instantly recall what you want to talk about, try Tony Buzan's concept of mindmapping. Here's a QR code to show you dozens of examples.

http://bit.ly/2GqyjvG

This is a hand-drawn and visual "map" of exactly what you're going to cover in a presentation. You can glance down at it on the lectern at any time to recall what comes next.

Mindmapping is one of the most underutilized tools for use when you want to move your speaking anxiety into the Blue Zone. It's easy to create. It's easy to follow. It's even easy to recall in your minds-eye. Usually an image triggers recollection faster than asking yourself, "What's the next slide?" or "What's the next idea?"

So I encourage you to research mindmapping as a way not only to recall talking points but also to organize them in the first place. All you need is a piece of paper and a pencil.

12: PERSONAL ROUTINE

Every one of us has a conscious or unconscious routine for most things you do in life—how you get up in the morning, brush your teeth, eat your breakfast, and so on. What I'm suggesting to you here is that you build a personal routine of what you do in the moments just before you speak.

What is important is that you design your own routine using some of the tools already mentioned and some yet to be covered. Then fine-tune it until it becomes your go-to method. If you practice it, you will notice a difference in how speaking anxiety affects you. You'll figure out what your personal routine is and what works for you. Maybe all you need to do is run up on stage just like Ringo Starr.

As a brief example, part of my personal routine is to make sure all the technology— lighting, sound, and visuals—is working in the room where I will be speaking. I have trouble sleeping the night before a talk if I can't first get into the room to see what it is like. If I can't, I usually arrive at least an hour before the talk to walk the stage and get comfortable with the surroundings. My routine is flexible, and I adjust it based on the job at hand.

13: REMEMBER, BE HERE NOW

One of the most useful things you can do to harness your speaking anxiety is to remind yourself of these three words: "Be here now." You need to be here now to help your brain stop projecting the possible future. It's too easy to anticipate an adverse outcome and engage in negative thought processes just when you need to be clear-minded. Reminding yourself to "Be here now" will help you stop predicting the future and get your mind back to the task at hand.

Remember, Be Here Now is one of my favorite books from the 1970s. I placed it on my shelf where I could see its spine almost every day. To be honest, I never actually read the book. I bought it because of the title. That was all I needed from the book, a reminder to "Be here now." To this day it has been a beneficial mantra to help me center and focus on the present where all things are possible.

When I feel speaking anxiety and say "Be here now" to myself, it instantly brings me back to the present where I can concentrate on the presentation's goal. The speaking anxiety we all feel tends to come from wondering what people will think of us or trying to predict the future. Thoughts like those will kill enthusiasm more quickly than just about anything else.

By saying these three words out loud to yourself, you can remind yourself to be in the now. It's going to be all right. This simple concept helps if your speaking anxiety starts going off in the Red Zone.

14: ADVANCED BREATHING TECHNIQUE

I've talked a lot about breathing because it is the first and most essential aspect of harnessing speaking anxiety. If you are not breathing correctly, your brain is not getting enough oxygen; you won't sound as authentic, honest, and convincing as you could be. The stress of speaking in front of people or to a group online will always have a physical effect on you depending on the situation.

However, if your speaking anxiety is severe and it is keeping you from success, I want you to know about a technique they teach first responders—police, fire fighters, military personnel—for the inevitable times when their senses are confused and they are in a panic state or their anxiety causes a debilitated reaction.

It's called Tactical Breathing, also known as Combat Breathing. It can be done anywhere at any time, and people do not need to know you are doing it. The way it works is that you inhale for a steady count of four, hold your breath for that same count of 4 or amount of time, and then slowly exhale for a count of four while you say something "Relax" to yourself. Repeat this tactical breathing 3-5 times or until you feel a sense of calm when your heart rate slows down. Practice this sequence a few times at home or in the office so that when you need it you'll know what to do.

15: MOOD INDUCER

Without a doubt the most straightforward and powerful tool for harnessing speaking anxiety is what psychologists call a "mood inducer." What's that, you ask? It can be anything that induces a positive mood or feeling in your mind. It could be a sound. It could be a perfume or cologne or a type of flower. It could be the taste of a particular food or drink. For many, myself included, the best mood inducer is music.

My bet is that you have at least one piece of music which, when you hear it, causes goosebumps on your arms or makes the back of your neck tingle. It's usually associated with a movie or a peak experience in your life. Recalling that particular piece of music in your mind makes you feel powerful, unstoppable, and confident before you speak. You can play it in the car or on the way to the office. If you are lucky enough to have walk-on music the AV people play as you approach the stage, you might think of using your mood inducer. The audience does not need to know what it does for you because they will feel it when you speak.

Using a mood inducer works like magic because it instantly creates a better state of mind for speaking. It also helps you drown out your inner-voice predicting the future and orients you more into the here and now.

http://bit.ly/2vouqCp

I use the theme song from the original *Rocky* movie called "Gonna Fly Now" every time I walk up to speak with people. That particular piece of music causes instant goosebumps on my arms. I picked that song to induce a mood that makes me feel unstoppable. When you listen to music, you tend to forget about the future, especially if you crank up the volume.

16: TOUCH

Touch can be a quick way to harness speaking anxiety. If all you do is to wrap your arms around yourself and squeeze a bit, it might reduce your anxiety. Touch should also help you focus on the present moment. This technique comes from acting and improvisation classes.

If you're freaking out about what lies ahead, you may regain control by just rubbing your arm or grabbing both hands and squeezing them together a few times to remind you that you are alive and breathing. No one will even notice.

You can even say to yourself, "It's going to be all right. I'm ready and excited to be here." You might even get a hug from somebody else. It all depends on who you are and how you accept and react to physical contact from other people.

17: VIRTUAL CONSOLE

One of the tools you can take with you wherever you go and use whenever you speak is your own personally configured console. It's virtual, so it can be anything you want it to be and designed to your specifications. It's like a control panel for your speaking anxiety. This is something sitting right in front of you that no one else can see.

One of the reasons a virtual console is essential is that your listeners will go through different levels of response and energy during your talk no matter what the length. The console you design for yourself can have dials, sliders, and perhaps even a digital readout for adjusting how you are speaking.

To use your Virtual Console, if you need to increase the volume a bit, virtually slide the volume bar up. If you are getting carried away, showing too much energy, and the feedback loop you created with your audience is beginning to break down, adjust the console's energy lever accordingly. The same goes for all other dials and levers you have.

With a virtual console at your disposal, you should be able to handle just about any situation that arises when you speak. You can always add more function to your console when and if you need it. It's entirely up to you, but I suggest that you start with a volume slider, a pacing lever, and an enthusiasm dial with an indicator needle that you can adjust while speaking.

Feel free to continually adjust the items you have on your virtual console. It is yours to do with whatever you choose. If you need more dials and levers, add them. If you find you are not using the ones you already "installed" remove or replace them with something else.

Before I leave this topic, there are even more ways you can use your virtual console to help you deal with speaking anxiety.

The amount of energy involved in speaking, whether it's in front of ten people at your office or before a large audience at a conference, is a bit like show business. When you go to a play or watch a movie and get vicariously involved, aren't the characters doing precisely what an effective public speaker does? Don't you feel something based on their delivery, vocal range, and body language?

There's nothing wrong with doing that to persuade and influence people. It can be a bit of an act in the beginning until you get comfortable with what you want to say and how you want to say it. The best speakers know this and use it to get their audiences involved. Eventually your "acting" becomes very authentic and believable.

I look at what we do as speakers and presenters as if it were a sport. I realize that sports metaphors are overused in business, but speaking is a sport. When you see it in this light, you may offer your audience a different experience by showing them the real you, even if it's a bit of an act! When I am finished speaking, whether for 15 minutes or six hours, I feel as though I've been running a marathon. I am enthusiastic about the talk and, more importantly, the audience. Did I make my audience the hero in my talk? Hopefully so.

18: ACCENT REDUCTION MANAGEMENT

Accents can sometimes cause anxiety not only for the speaker but also for the audience. A substantial percentage of my clients have accents and struggle with English. It is sometimes hard for them to present prepared material but even harder to handle questions from the audience. Most difficult of all is knowing where and how to put enthusiasm into a delivery while struggling to be sure you are saying things that make sense and that people can understand.

Accent is a beautiful part of who you are, so long as listeners can understand the words that you're saying in English. If they can't, your message is not being heard, and it probably won't have the impact you want.

Watch this short segment of comedian Gabriel Iglesias in which he illustrates how funny yet serious speaking in English can be when it is not one's first language.

http://bit.ly/2IHaLW2

If you were not able to watch the short video, here's a transcript. However, watching it will be more informative because you will hear the tone changes in his voice and see the expressions on his face.

"I think the most impressive thing about that fight was probably the interviews. The interviews are what were really entertaining. For me, if you're going to interview a Mexican fighter, just let the fighter do the interview in Spanish in his native tongue. Don't make him speak English. In Spanish, Canelo sounded like a killer. The guys on ESPN speak in Spanish. And then he came out all killer, and his words in Spanish sounded powerful, compelling, and believable. In translation, 'He's going to die.' It sounded like a good interview, but then they put his ass in English, and the whole fight is different.

'This is Phil Stevens here live for ESPN Sports. We have here with me today Canelo Álvarez who's going to face Floyd Money Mayweather this weekend in Los Vegas, Nevada, at the MGM Grand on Pay-Per-View. Canelo, what's your strategy against Floyd Money Mayweather?' And then he talks, and he kills it, right? 'Uh, well, I am going to hit him like this, and then I'm going to hit him like this, and then he's going to, *Como se dice piso*? He's going to hit the floor and then stand down like that. Okay?'"

I get it. When a non-native speaker has to rely on English, it's tough to bring out all the emphasis, enthusiasm, pauses, and right words. I deal with people all the time who are in this situation. I don't speak any language other than English, so I don't know what this difficulty is like, but here's what I have learned.

First, audiences will understand your challenges when English is not your first language. They always get it. When you come to Silicon Valley and have, say, a Norwegian accent, people will note things that don't click idiomatically. For example, in some parts of the world you'll hear, "Could you please take a decision by tonight so we can move on with this please?" Everybody knows what that means.

However, if you say that in Silicon Valley and some other places in the West, people think, "Wait a minute. We don't 'take' decisions here. We 'make' decisions." Just a little word like that makes you sound different. However, we all do understand, and we allow it. It's okay. You don't have to say things perfectly for people to understand what you mean, especially if you allow your authenticity to be conveyed at the same time.

Second, if you don't know the right words, learn them. If you don't speak English well, find somebody to help you learn the words that you need to say and get better at it. I know that it's easy for me to say that as a person who speaks only English. The real key may be that you just need to say less. However, make sure that you learn those things you need to communicate and articulate well. Also, ask more questions.

Third, when somebody asks you a question and you're not quite sure what was asked because you can't translate it fast enough, you may need to ask the person to repeat it. However, I'm going to give you a hint: Don't just say, "Can you repeat your question, please?" because many people will repeat the same words. So you need to say something like, "Could you please repeat your question but use different words because I'm not quite getting what you're asking me?"

Then you might have a better chance of understanding what someone is asking. By the way, if there is someone in the room who can translate the question, it is totally within reason to ask for some help. Not being fully fluent in English does not show weakness unless you make it seem like a weakness.

Finally, there is something concrete you can do to help with your accent so that an audience will be able to clearly understand every word you speak no matter where you are from or how heavy your accent may be. This is a topic of which most people are unaware. It's called "Accent Reduction Management," and it is taught in ESL classes or by specialists such as Scottie Spurzem, the English Language Coach, in San Francisco, California.

http://bit.ly/2VXUzTZ

She will whip you into shape in a few weeks. I've seen her tutor somebody from Italy who came to the States to speak English at a conference. I couldn't understand 90% of the words he was saying one month before the scheduled presentation. It sounded like one long sentence. In the following video you will hear the transformation in the Italian speaker who worked with Scottie.

http://bit.ly/2viu0gs

So when you speak in English and listeners say, "Could you repeat that?" or "What did you say?" consider getting some coaching help. Speech departments at some universities can help you with this too. When you articulate all your words clearly, you have a better chance of captivating your audience and getting them to take action.

19: START WITH WHY

I started this book with why we all experience speaking anxiety to varying degrees. Let's end with the same point. I am talking about the "Golden Circle" that Simon Sinek introduced to the world in 2009 through his TEDx presentation. If you have not seen this talk, please watch it now before going any further. The next two chapters will make more sense after you have heard his 18-minute talk.

http://bit.ly/2uOeCIv

If you consider yourself a leader or want to become a leader in the future, Sinek's talk should resonate because you know how to engage an audience at an emotional level based on science and research. Following the "Golden Circle" and starting with "why" when you speak should help you to harness speaking anxiety.

A book titled *Start with Why* goes with the talk if you want to read more about it. I have been a big proponent of it ever since I first watched the talk in 2009. By the way, it is the most viewed TED talk in history.

20: FIND YOUR WHY

Finding your why is the ultimate tool for harnessing speaking anxiety. If you know what your "why" is each time you speak, you will sound more compelling and perhaps be more memorable. When you know your "why," you will find it easier to speak from your heart rather than your mind. Plus, you won't feel so much like an imposter.

At the age of 19 a self-help book taught me that if I helped enough people get what they want out of their lives, I would live a fulfilled life. I believed the author and pretty much lived my whole adult life with this as my "why." I also was influenced by my mother who was always helping people in various ways. I've incorporated assisting others in my day-to-day life in any way possible. I help people with directions. I help them shovel their snow. I sometimes even paid for cars behind me in the old days before toll tags, as a random act of kindess.

Today at age 61 I can tell you that the author of that book was correct. By helping others without expecting anything in return, I wake up in the morning and go to sleep at night feeling fulfilled. If you ask what my "why" is, I would answer, "To help people get more out of their lives so that they can be happier." I hope that I've helped you with the tools in this book so far.

My "why" became even more apparent to me when I read a book that came out in September 2017. *Find Your Why* is a step-by-step practical guide that answers all the questions not addressed in *Start with Why*. The most interesting point this book made was that all of our individual "why's" are in our past and not in our future. You already know what you need to do in order to change and start living your "why."

All you need to do is to sit down with somebody you trust and use the step-by-step process outlined in this book to discover your "why." You don't have to create your "why." It's already in your past. The book can also help you to identify your company's "why" and how it is not always congruent with your own. When you know your "why," your public speaking will change for the better.

When I read *Find Your Why*, two things happened to me. The first is that I realized my "why" had changed when I started my own business at age 50. I was living a happy, healthy, and fulfilled life. What *Find Your Why* made me realize was that my "why" had become: "To inspire people like you to help other people get more out of their lives so that we all live more fulfilled lives together." This is why I get up every morning happy and go to sleep every night fulfilled. The second thing that happened was that I realized *Find Your Why* perfectly complements Dale Carnegie's *How to Win Friends and Influence People*. These two books are the most influential self-help books that have helped me become the person I am today.

When you live your "why," your speaking opportunities will be more interesting for you and your audience. You'll be able to talk more from the heart. People will generally respect, admire, and believe in you more. Living your why is one sure way you become a more authentic, honest, and real person. It can make every day more fulfilling for yourself and even those people in your life.

PART 1: CONCLUSION

Let's go back to where we started. We've acknowledged that we all have speaking anxiety and that it's not going away. That black stallion representing your speaking anxiety is going to be with you for the rest of your life, so accept it, harness it, and love it. You can always ask yourself this question in the minutes leading up to a speaking engagement: "What's the worst thing that can happen?" Take your time in easing into regular use of tools to help you. Don't expect to wake up tomorrow able to do everything we've talked about here.

You can't use all 18 tools at once. Pick the ones that resonate with you and the ones you want to try first. I gave you this toolbox so that you can choose the ones best suited for you and your situation. Some tools you'll use all the time, of course, such as controlled and proper breathing.

Take your time practicing harnessing your speaking anxiety. It could take weeks or even months. Go easy on yourself and don't expect overnight success. The more speaking you do, the more you can experiment with these tools. The more you use them, the more places you'll find for their use. I tell people, "We all have butterflies, but mine are flying in formation and you can get your to do the same."

Take deliberate steps in working on your speaking anxiety. If you have to make a little card to remind yourself of the things you want to do, take it with you. Write it on the back of your hand, if you have to, or put a yellow sticky note on your laptop. Over time you will see that you can harness your speaking anxiety and make it work for you rather than against you.

Practice using these tools before you expect excellence from yourself. Try them out on different people in different situations. Find more opportunities to speak so that you can experiment to learn what works and what doesn't work. Even comedians practice on real audiences before they can repeat a joke with the right words, pauses, and facial expressions to evoke a predictable or repeatable emotional response.

When you are ready, Part 2 is next. Turn the page to begin learning how you can more easily connect emotionally with your audience.

PART 2: INTRODUCTION

Now that you have learned 18 tools you can use to harness your speaking anxiety, it's time to explore proven ways to connect emotionally with your audience. Once again, I promise only solid nourishment and no empty calories.

All right, let's get going. Since Simon Sinek has tried since 2009 to get people around the globe to start with their "why," why don't we follow his lead as we did earlier in this book? Let's begin with, "Why connect emotionally with your audience? Why do that?"

We could spend hours talking about the whys and the results of what happens when you connect emotionally with your audience. However, I think you intuitively know why this connection is important.

The following quote from Maya Angelou, an American poet, memoirist, and civil rights activist, sums up this part of the book:

> *"I've learned that people will*
> *forget what you've said,*
> *people will forget what you did,*
> *but people will never forget how*
> *you made them feel."*

She's correct, right?

I am confident that you have several experiences, talks, or presentations that you recall were very memorable because the speaker made you to *feel* something. Perhaps you even now can feel what you felt back then. If so, you know the power of what can happen when you take the time to connect emotionally with an audience of any size.

Let's explore what you can do and use this quotation from Angelou as inspiration for taking on the challenge of connecting emotionally with your audiences for a purpose. This section of the book will provide you ten tools, techniques, and tips toward that end. However, affecting emotions comes responsibility. It is essential to think about your audience and be purposeful in your use of these tools.

Ready? Let's get started. Please put your headphones on (if you're in public) and turn up the volume! It is time to set the stage and get started with this first video:

http://bit.ly/2K2nWmC

No text accompanies this video. It is the original movie trailer for *Rocky* (1976). I will explain why I asked you to do this later on.

There is also a photo ("The Afghan Girl") I want you to see. Please spend 30-60 seconds looking into her eyes:

http://bit.ly/2FPJmy5

Thank you for doing that again. I will explain.

This is NOT complicated stuff. The concepts and techniques are simple and will generally elicit emotions from your audience. This is a simple book with simple concepts and simple techniques. You will be able to use the tools shared here immediately in some cases, but others will take practice and experimentation.

Most people overthink this topic. You are connecting with people on an emotional level all of the time. However, you can do it better, more effectively, and with greater purpose especially when you need or want to be more persuasive.

So let's start with some research related to emotions. I have done homework and it appears that no one agrees on exactly how many emotions we all have. It's six, seven, or eight, so they say.

Here are "the" seven human emotions identified by experts:

1. Anger
2. Contempt
3. Disgust
4. Fear
5. Happiness

6. Sadness
7. Surprise

However, I've never thought that this list is complete or representative of all my emotional experiences. So while doing my research, I found a better answer.

UC Berkeley did a study on human emotions in 2017, and they produced research with additional distinctions. According to their study, humans have 27 emotions.

Here is the UC Berkeley list:

1. Admiration
2. Adoration
3. Aesthetic Appreciation
4. Amusement
5. Anger
6. Anxiety
7. Awe
8. Awkwardness
9. Boredom
10. Calmness
11. Confusion
12. Craving
13. Disgust
14. Empathetic Pain
15. Entrancement
16. Excitement
17. Fear
18. Horror
19. Interest
20. Joy

21. Nostalgia
22. Relief
23. Romance
24. Sadness
25. Satisfaction
26. Sexual Desire
27. Surprise

Let's do a quick test?

Please watch the video below now. I want you to watch it first before going any further into this book. Ready?

Watch this YouTube video ("Distracted Driving"):

http://bit.ly/2IbQ1W1

QUIZ #1: Thank you for watching that video. How many of the 27 emotions did you experience while watching? Here's the list again:

Admiration, Adoration, Aesthetic Appreciation, Amusement, Anger, Anxiety, Awe, Awkwardness, Boredom, Calmness, Confusion, Craving, Disgust, Empathetic Pain, Entrancement, Excitement, Fear, Horror, Interest, Joy, Nostalgia, Relief, Romance, Sadness, Satisfaction, Sexual Desire, and Surprise.

My guess is that you felt one or more emotions on this list. See how easy it is to connect emotionally with your audience?

All right, let's change the mood a bit, okay?

Watch this YouTube video ("The Power of Not Giving Up"):

http://bit.ly/2Ka8eWD

There are not many words in this video, and the ones you hear are somewhat inaudible. Wait for it: "Okay! Okay! Whoa! Yeah! Yeah! Yeah! Yeah!"

QUIZ #2: How many of the 27 emotions did you experience during this video?

Admiration, Adoration, Aesthetic Appreciation, Amusement, Anger, Anxiety, Awe, Awkwardness, Boredom, Calmness, Confusion, Craving, Disgust, Empathetic Pain, Entrancement, Excitement, Fear, Horror, Interest, Joy, Nostalgia, Relief, Romance, Sadness, Satisfaction, Sexual Desire, and Surprise.

Do you see how easy it was to get you to feel more positive emotions, and this was much shorter than the "Distracted Driving" video, right? Do you see how I was able to get you to cry or feel sadness as well as joy and happiness, and all within minutes of each other? Moreover, I wasn't even doing the talking or sharing a personal, heartfelt story. This is partly why I keep reminding you that most people are overthinking the concept of how to connect emotionally with your audience.

All right. It's time to go through the 10 proven ways you can connect emotionally with your audience. It is important that you think of these ten ways as tools in a toolbox. You can use one or more of these tools at the same time or at the right spots in your presentation or talk.

This is not an exhaustive list of techniques. However, it does contain some of the easiest and most straightforward methods you can use to evoke emotional responses in your audience.

Please keep in mind that when you evoke emotions in your audience, you have a responsibility to those people. You cannot leave them hanging! I encourage you to experiment with the tools in this book first and then invent your own. Be sure to test your ideas on real people before blindly using them on an audience.

This part of the book is going to be a reasonably quick read. The truth is that I've already used all 10 proven ways to connect emotionally with you, my audience, multiple times throughout this book. Most of them were used again in the introduction to Part 2 as a real-world example!

Let's see if you can identify where, when, and how I did this after you know the 10 proven ways to connect emotionally with your audience starting with the first tool, which is music.

21: MUSIC

The first way you can connect emotionally with your audience is with music. Music is universal. It is so simple, elegant, and often compelling. It can be used intentionally with an expected result, applies to every culture and works everywhere in the world.

http://bit.ly/2vouqCp

Earlier I asked you to watch and listen to the Rocky trailer primarily for the music. That Bill Conte track titled "Gonna Fly Now" usually gets people energized, excited, or ready to rumble no matter where in the world I use it. Did you feel it?

The music and the scenes of Rocky Balboa training for the big day in the ring are recognized worldwide. It was the #1 grossing film that year, and I watched it four times on the day it came out, hiding in the men's room until the next show started. The movie made a significant impression on me at 19 years old, and it created a powerful metaphor for my life.

My guess is that it elicited some emotional response from you too. I still get goosebumps when I hear that theme music, and the movie came out over 40 years ago!

So why not start with some music in your next talk or meeting? You can have it playing as people arrive. Perhaps the choice of music you use to start your talk, lecture, or meeting will set the mood without your even having to say anything. All you need to do is to arrive early enough to get your kit set up and sound-tested from the projector, LCD panel, or speakers you bring.

Use popular and known music that you are confident generates some feelings in your audience without your having to do anything except make sure it is not too loud. It's effortless to access music today on the Internet.

If you don't have a theme in mind for the music selection and you're looking for something that can work in just about any situation, search YouTube for "The Piano Guys." They are my favorite go-to music videos to play before any talk or workshop. People are mesmerized by these musicians, especially when they see and hear them for the first time.

Here is my favorite Piano Guys video to play for any audience:

http://bit.ly/2UuVnCj

22: PICTURES

Pictures are the next proven way you can connect emotionally with your audience. There are countless pictures out there for you to use to help convey to an audience what it is you want them to feel.

In the beginning of this book I included a picture of a wild-looking and beautiful black stallion for two reasons. The reason I used the stallion as a metaphor for your speaking anxiety is to help you remember what's inside you when you speak and how to harness it. Is it working for you? Does the image stand out in your mind? Hopefully, yes.

In the introduction to Part 2, I had you gaze at the famous *National Geographic* photograph of "The Afghan Girl," Sharbat Gulafrom from 1984, the girl with the intense green eyes. If you have not seen it yet, please check it out now.

http://bit.ly/2FPJmy5

I used that picture because it is one of the most famous and recognizable photos ever to appear on the cover of *National Geographic* and it's incredibly captivating. It's mesmerizing. It's moving. It always gets people in my audiences staring intently and feeling something.

If you have seen this picture, my guess is that it moved you. You felt something when you looked at her eyes, didn't you? People always respond to this picture in some emotional way. I can usually see it written all over their faces. Even if you have seen it in the past, it's hard not to wonder what she was thinking at the moment that photo was taken.

During my workshops I always use a compelling picture such as "The Afghan Girl" on my title slide, but I choose one relevant to my talk. Since the image is usually staring people in the face for a while, it provides an excellent opportunity to catch people's attention and perhaps get them emotionally connected before you even start speaking.

The challenge is to select pictures that either directly relate to your topic or illustrate your point or message. They can be pictures that you have drawn or taken yourself, or pictures that you buy from stock websites. You can also download them from Google or Bing. In addition to pictures, you can get a similar emotional effect from illustrations, word clouds, hand-drawn images, charts and graphs, infographics, pictographs, comics, animated GIFs, and even some icons.

After searching for images, filter your search results based on the licensing from the owner to make legal use of the pictures instead of "borrowing" them.

23: VIDEOS

Videos are an extremely effective way to connect emotionally with your audience. I started the introduction to Part 2 by having you watch the *Rocky* movie trailer. That was an illustration of how using a video can get your audience emotionally connected to you and your topic. Even if you have seen the movie, my guess is that by the end of the trailer you were feeling some emotion.

Let's move on to the "Distracted Driving" video sponsored by www.itcanwait.com. You do not need to play the video again because I am confident that you remember exactly how you felt when Jacy said, "I did not have my daddy to walk me down the aisle when I got married."

Didn't you feel something more deeply at that moment in the video than in the other parts? It was a very compelling thing to say, and Jacy said it without any tears but with the power of someone with a message to all people who need to listen and take it to heart.

Finally, the last video I had you watch was "The Power of Not Giving Up." What that video demonstrated is how one father helped his young daughter to learn the lesson of the power of not giving up. It's evident that she has tried box-jumping many times. You can tell by differences in the lighting, clothing, and situation. It seems honest, real, and emotionally charged, especially at the end.

Didn't you feel one or more positive emotions when that little girl finally landed the jump and high-fived her encouraging dad? I know I did, and I still do every time I see the video.

Do you see how using a carefully selected video can evoke an emotion? So long as the video you are using is relevant to your topic or talk, it can work wonders. Remember, the choice of video can demonstrate a specific point you are trying to make with your audience, or it can be more generally metaphorical. You may need to explain why you chose a particular video. However, the most critical part of playing a video for an audience is to be sure that the sound can be heard by everyone in the room or online.

As you have experienced throughout your life, videos and movies can often leave lasting impressions, and they have the power to motivate people to take action. They get people to stop in their tracks, focus and listen, watch and react. So use them wisely. You may be surprised at how quickly they work for you and your audience.

Finding relevant videos online for your topic is not hard these days. There are hundreds of excellent TED and TEDx talks you can use as literal or metaphorical examples, along with many other user-generated content examples. You merely need to spend a little time searching for them.

If you can't find what you need, make your own, or visit a website where professional videographers sell clips of their work. Then you can stitch together your video using professionally shot clips to connect emotionally with your audience. There are even websites now where you can upload video clips and edit them inside the browser without having to know much about video editing or installing any software.

24: QUOTES

Quotes are amazingly simple to find and use to connect emotionally with your audience. The quotations can be from a famous person or source. However, even anonymous quotes can work wonders.

I started this book with a quotation from Maya Angelou, "I've learned that people will forget what you've said, people will forget what you did, but people will never forget how you made them feel." The statement more than likely made you consider the idea that connecting with people on an emotional level is probably a good thing.

In every language and culture there are excellent, provocative, and insightful quotes from which to choose. Whether they're directly related to a topic you're going to talk about or more broadly metaphorical, quotes can be a fantastic hook or presentation opener to get people emotionally connected. See how simple this is?

You can even use quotes to "presuade," a word coined by Robert Cialdini in his 2016 book *PRE-SUASION: A Revolutionary Way to Influence and Persuade*, to encourage your audience to want to listen to what you have to say. If you put a quote in your invitation, on your event page, or in the subject line, you may find that you elicit curiosity from your audience before they even show up for your meeting, talk, or job interview.

25: START WITH WHY

When you start with why instead of what or how, you will automatically connect emotionally with your audience. Simon Sinek has proven through science and research that when you use "The Golden Circle" and "Start With Why," you are connecting to the limbic part of the listener's brain. This is the part of the brain that experiences emotions. Some people call this a gut feeling, hardly a new concept. Sinek simply made it understandable by the everyday person.

Sinek's talk on TEDx called "How Great Leaders Inspire Action" gives us some of the most powerful insights in recent years related to how our brain works when you are trying to persuade people to take action. Sinek shows us that if you start with "why" instead of "what," you will have a better chance of getting people emotionally connected to whatever it is you are saying, selling, or doing.

Apple's commercials start with why, and other successful companies and speakers are using the same "Start With Why" strategy. Try it with your friends and family, especially when you want them to take action. You can use "The Golden Circle" in just about any situation, even when a job interviewer asks, "Why should we hire you?"

Sinek followed his TEDx talk with a book titled *Start with Why* to give more details behind the concept of "The Golden Circle." If you have not seen his 2009 TEDx talk or read his book, you need to watch the video now. I promise that it will illuminate how the most effective leaders, speakers, and persuaders are using "The Golden Circle" to connect emotionally with their audiences.

If you have not seen Sinek's TEDx talk yet, please take the time now to watch this 18-minute YouTube video:

http://bit.ly/2uOeCIv

26: TIME

Time is precious. If you are looking for the easiest way to get people more interested instantly and leaning forward to listen in your talks, presentations, and meetings, try starting with time.

Time is becoming even more important every day. People are always wondering if their time will be well spent when listening to you speak. Everyone has something to do after you finish speaking. It would be best if you were not the reason they are late for the next item on their calendar. Letting your audience know when you will be finished can be the first sign that you care about your audience's time more than your own. Everyone appreciates that courtesy.

For example, assuming I have 30 minutes, here's a sample of how I start a meeting, presentation, or even telephone conversation: "Thank you so much for taking the time to listen to me talk about [fill in the blank]. Speaking of time, I expect this talk to take less than 15 minutes. That will leave 10 minutes for Q&A and 5 minutes for you to get to your next meeting. Let's get started."

Every time I start by addressing time, I can see people relax, lean forward, and in some cases even smile and nod their heads. This response from an audience usually indicates that they appreciate that I value their time. I can vouch for the results when you address time in the beginning because I have been doing this for over 40 years in thousands of situations.

When you tell people you appreciate their time, thank them for their time, make sure things start on time, and end on time, they tend to enjoy and value their time with you more. It is easier to connect emotionally with your audience by respecting time than just about anything else in this book.

You can also address time by verifying the time you think you have with your audience during your opening remarks. A simple way to do that is to say something like, "Thank you so much for taking the time to listen to my talk. Speaking of time, do we still have 30 minutes together or has something changed since we arranged this meeting?"

If the answer is yes, you can quickly respond with something like, "Okay. Thank you. My plan here is to talk for 15 minutes, leaving ten minutes for Q&A and five minutes for you to get to your next meeting. Let's get started."

If the answer is no, you may have just saved the day. Perhaps something significant came up just minutes before you arrived for your talk, and your audience needs to get to another important call or meeting following yours. So now you can begin by saying something like, "Thank you for letting me know about the urgent call you need to make at the bottom of the hour. With that in mind I promise that I will finish in time for you to get to that call and perhaps even make a quick pit-stop for coffee, tea, or the lavatory. Let's get started."

If you prefer to verify the time you think you have with your audience before you step up in front of them, ask your event organizer to confirm the time you have with the audience. Then you can start your talk by saying something like, "I checked with Jane, and she informed me that we have until the bottom of the hour for this meeting. Let's get started."

Alternatively, you can say something like this: "After speaking with Jane, I was informed that you have an urgent call to make at the bottom of the hour. With that in mind, I promise that I will finish in time for you to get to that call. Let's get started."

There is another technique I like to use that I encourage you to try. I will often start my talks by thanking people for their time and then promising them I will not waste it. I start this way because I know that their time is precious, that they are preoccupied, and that they probably want to be somewhere else. Some people will call me out on this and tell me that I promised the audience I wouldn't waste their time because I probably will, but they are mistaken when it comes to my talks.

I know that there are cultural norms and differences when it comes to starting promptly. For example, at UC Berkeley there is "Berkeley Time," an actual policy at the university mandating that classes start 10 minutes later than their scheduled time to allow students to make it across campus. Your culture or company may have its own norm.

In general, however, people do not like it when you start late, especially when they have arrived early or promptly. I grew up with a mother who taught me either to be on time or to let her know I would be late and why. That is one reason I always appreciate it when people start meetings, talks, and conferences when scheduled. It makes me "feel" good that they respect my time even if, for example, the mayor of the city has not arrived yet.

Speaking of being late, I suggest that you show appreciation to those people who arrived on time. If you need to start late, you can take the opportunity to connect emotionally with the people in the room or online at the start time by saying something like, "Thank you all for being on time or even early to this talk. I appreciate the time you are giving me today. I have been asked to delay the start. Please take a moment and get yourself a fresh cup of coffee or tea, and we'll begin promptly in 10 minutes.

Why do this? Because audiences often contain people like me. When things start late, I always feel as though I am not that important. I start having a negative response to the speaker and the situation. I arrived on time, after all, so why the delayed start? Let your audience know why there is a delay even if it is a technical one. It happens. However, having listeners angry with you is not the way you want anyone in your audience to feel before you even start.

Of course, I hope you know I realize I am not that important in the grand scheme of things. But remember to show appreciation to those people like me who are right there in front of you or online waiting for your talk. Don't miss out on this opportunity. You never know who is in your audience or who may walk out because they felt their time was being wasted.

If you cannot tell from the length of this chapter, time is one of my pet peeves whether I am the one speaking or the one in the audience. Nothing is more important to someone with a commitment or engagement after your talk than the time they have to get to it. While we tend to think our topic or talk is essential, I've learned that there is always a fundamental question in the minds of your listeners: "When is this going to be over?" or "Is this going to be a waste of my time?

Finally, there are two more ways you can use the time to connect emotionally with your audience. The first is to thank your audience once more for its time as you are wrapping up, but make it sound sincere and not like an afterthought. The second way is to give your audience the gift of time by trying to finish early. If you have achieved your goal before your maximum allotment of scheduled time, give those extra minutes back to your audience, and they will remember you all day long. Doing so will trigger feelings similar to the way a gift works with people—surprise, excitement, and usually joy.

Serendipity can also take place when people have a chance to mingle instead of rushing off or picking up their devices. Very few people appreciate how important time is to their audience. I guarantee that you will see smiles all around when you give people the gift of extra time. It's so easy to do this, but most people think they have to fill up their entire time with more "stuff." Usually they don't.

27: FATAL FOUR EMOTIONAL APPEALS

Using the "Fatal Four Emotional Appeals" can be a sneaky but very effective way to connect emotionally with your audience. These appeals are based on fundamental human nature. However, they require careful consideration before use with an audience.

More than 45 years ago I picked up a copy of Roy Garn's *The Magic Power of Emotional Appeal,* a paperback no longer in print, despite being a top selection in six national book clubs. The book is about how to get people to want to listen to you. It taught me how to break through the preoccupations that everyone wrestles with all of the time.

The book's "Fatal Four Emotional Appeals" are broken down into these categories: Self-Preservation, Recognition, Romance, and Money. While each category involves a high emotional response for many different reasons, two consistently stimulate reactions of high intensity: Self-Preservation and Recognition. The former elicits the highest and most consistent response of all.

By understanding the big "preoccupation-breaking" emotional appeals, you can capture an audience's attention, stimulate an emotional reaction, and command a desired response. I can vouch for this because I have been using these "Fatal Four Emotional Appeals" ever since I read the book in the late 1970s. Since human nature has not changed much since the book was published in 1960, Garn's insights still apply and work like magic today.

Truly captivating an audience by using the "Fatal Four Emotional Appeals" is all about breaking people's preoccupations. Their preoccupations may range from financial concerns to family plans, personal well-being to daydreams about the future, and immediate tasks to be done at work or home. Until you find the right emotional appeal, all of these concerns will take precedence over your message in your listener's mind.

Here are the basics behind each of the "Fatal Four Emotional Appeals."

1. SELF-PRESERVATION. Personal safety and security, of course, are inherent to everyone in your audience.

An appeal to self-preservation motivates audience members to listen intently. Triggering responses to personal safety, fear, hope, danger, pain, injury, or even death will prompt people to feel something. Self-preservation has a high impact in other relationships as well.

When you claim that you have a hidden key to longer, more enjoyable life, your audience is biologically predisposed to listen and be captivated. As an example, this appeal can be used by beginning with a statistic about how many members of the audience are at risk of a chronic heart condition that your product can mitigate in some way.

This appeal can also be used as a claim to increase quality of life by streamlining processes that make life easier and more enjoyable. Both of these opening appeals fall in the category of self-preservation.

2. RECOGNITION. Why do we always want to be seen in the best light, appearing confident in photos rather than getting caught in an unflattering angle? We all want to be seen as though we have it all together.

Recognition as an emotional appeal compels us all, not just to look successful but in hopes that the appearance of success will make us *feel* like a success. Although its degree varies from person to person, the desire for accomplishment and recognition is embedded in all of us.

The simplest way to use this emotional appeal effectively is to say thank you. You must be sure that your tone of voice is honest, humble, and authentic when you say something like, "Thank you so much for taking the time to join me today. I appreciate all of your ideas and thoughts. If it weren't for you, I would not be feeling as confident as I do about the meeting with my boss tomorrow. Thank you once again.

Of course, recognition comes in hundreds of other ways such as a raise in your salary, an extra day off with pay, a free lunch, a party in your honor, and a handwritten note of thanks. Or perhaps your boss singles you out in front of the entire company to praise you for something you did that had a significant effect on the firm's bottom line.

3. ROMANCE. Have you ever seen an advertisement for a tropical getaway? Of course, you have. Well, the only place you'll see an appeal to romance nearly as strong is in a commercial for wedding rings.

Perhaps this is useful because the idea of lying on a beach with a fancy drink doesn't seem as great when experienced in solitude. However, by seeing romantic couples on the beach, in the spa, and at posh restaurants, viewers are captivated by the biological desire for intimate relationships. Moreover, this does not work only for singles. Those in committed relationships tend to feel the same way.

Romance as an emotional appeal is divided into three parts: sexual attraction and the desire for lasting relationships, future promise, and new experience.

Attraction and Desire: While some aspects of sex might seem to fall under self-preservation, attraction and desire are associated with the appeal of romance. This appeal calls on our desire to be with charming, attractive partners, but it also stems from the desire to be recognized as an attractive partner yourself. Emotional attraction and desire are not something that we can see or touch. However, once awakened, this appeal is the only thing on which we can focus. Romance is a prime preoccupation that can unlock padlocks of reason by outperforming all other appeals. This is one of the main reasons why beautiful people are typically used in advertising.

Future Promise: While this appeal is rooted in and categorized as an appeal to romance, future promise extends to situations beyond that. It is a sure way to keep someone's attention focused on a future experience that offers recognition and money but sometimes also self-preservation. This appeal gives your audience something to look forward to with excitement and enthusiasm. It is this appeal that leaves people daydreaming about what their life would be like with your technique, product, service, or knowledge. Using a romantic appeal like a future promise at the outset of a presentation (perhaps coupled with an imaginative story to emphasize the point) will give your audience a reason to connect emotionally and pay close attention.

New Experience: This appeal comes across when you show an audience what is truly unique about yourself, your product, or your service. Mirroring every other presentation, product, or story your audience has encountered will do nothing to build rapport, interest, or emotional connection. But don't just think that you're different. *Show them.* Your actions and stories speak infinitely more loudly than your claim to be different if no one can even remember what you said in the first place. New experience is likely a serious appeal for investors because, as much as they're looking to invest in tried and true companies, no one suffers from FOMO (fear of missing out) on the next big thing as much as investors.

4. MONEY. A broken bookshelf on the side of the road with a handwritten sign reading "FREE" makes you look twice, right? Why does this word always seem to grab our attention?

What about stumbling upon a large amount of money in the pocket of a jacket or pair of pants you haven't worn in a while? No matter how much income you make every year, that found money always feels good. Money is often the most direct of the "Fatal Four Emotional Appeals."

Money indicates both security (an aspect of self-preservation) and prestige for most people. When time (another aspect of self-preservation) is money, people try to spend as little on the first to gain as much of the second. Nearly everyone wants money. There is so much uncertainty in the world that parting with money unnecessarily is terrifying and gaining more always seems overwhelmingly satisfying. Thus, your audience will always be receptive if you know how to prevent them from losing money or have an innovative (and legal) way of making more money.

So how do you identify the right emotional appeal or appeals to connect emotionally with your audience?

After reviewing each of the "Fatal Four Emotional Appeals," it's time to step back, observe, and analyze the words and actions of those to whom you are speaking. Take the time to discover when, where, and how you can use these emotional appeals to connect with people before, during, and after your presentation.

Rather than suggesting that you have something that can make your audience rich, secure, attractive, etc., try to be a bit softer in your tone by offering something that can make them richer, more secure, or more attractive. Many of your listeners might already feel wealthy, secure, and attractive. So inviting them to imagine an "increase" in their wealth, health, attractiveness, security, etc. reaches more people than asking them to imagine a static state that they may very well have already achieved.

People often ask me why these are called the "Fatal Four Emotional Appeals." I believe it is because when you use them they are "fatal" in that people cannot defend against their use. These Fatal Four, if used correctly, can instantly break through any preoccupation of your listeners and quickly connect with them on an emotional level.

Please be careful when you use these emotional appeals. They are very powerful, and they work. However, overuse can have an adverse affect of undermining your credibility. These appeals must be used with integrity. You can see it in people's eyes when you use them for the right reasons. Feel free to use one or a combination of appeals to connect with and keep the attention of your audience.

28: STORIES

Stories are an incredibly powerful way to connect emotionally with an audience. They don't have to be your personal stories. They can be third-party stories. They can be stories about a TED talk or user-generated content that you watched yesterday or last year. However, your stories won't just be stories told for the sake of telling stories. By factoring in emotions when you recount stories purposely, listeners feel what either you or people in the story felt making your delivery more powerful. Does this make sense?

Why are Ted Talks so mesmerizing? No one starts with an agenda slide, and no one starts by letting you know that they will be telling a story. They just start. Missing an opportunity as a speaker to use an effective story amounts to missing a chance to connect emotionally with your audience.

You are unlike anyone else, and no one else can tell your stories quite the way you can. Think of all the books, movies, and songs that have influenced the person you've become. It wasn't day-to-day experiences themselves that shaped you but the stories contained therein. Literature isn't a required course for no reason. Stories give us a window into a world that very rarely we would hear about anywhere else. If that doesn't get you excited, I don't know what will. Stories, especially honest, authentic, and real stories, work with all audiences.

It's important to note that the power of stories is not limitless. As much as you might love the details of your story, it's essential when telling it to an audience to avoid getting bogged down by the details. Focus on the most important and relevant aspects. It's okay to leave people a little bit curious. You can always use the rest of your talk to satisfy their curiosity or perhaps have a follow-up meeting or call.

I usually use the analogy of a movie trailer in talking about stories. When sharing stories with your listeners, keep in mind that they may only need the "movie trailer" version and not the movie. Your audience might not have signed on to see your whole movie yet. Consider giving them an encapsulated version of the story. Shorter, more concise communication is what people hope for in these busy times. Minimize what you say to achieve your goal, whether it is to connect emotionally with your audience or perhaps merely to make a point. It's not always about emotions!

Leaving a question floating out there and supplying an answer later will keep people engaged as you make your way toward a conclusion. The first ten or so seconds of a story are the most important because that is when your listener decides to keep listening or not. So please don't give an outline and don't announce that you're going to tell a story. Just tell the story.

With stories you have the opportunity to create a lasting impression in the minds of your listeners. Here are three reasons why stories work so well with audiences all around the world. I call them the 3 "Rs".

Relate: People can relate to stories almost instantly when they are relevant to a situation. They put themselves in your shoes or the shoes of people in the story. You are humanized. People grow up learning about and relating to the world through stories. They're an easy way to engage people of any age and a tried and true way to ensure that your listeners are paying attention.

Remember: People remember the things you share with them through stories. So tell them something you'd like them to remember. Bullet points are not for friends, and people don't remember them for as long as they will remember a compelling story.

Retell: People will retell the stories they hear, especially good ones. Word of mouth is still one of the most potent ways to get people to take action. Using stories is part of the secret to getting other people to share your mission or objective with their networks.

Here is an example of a story that has an incredibly powerful impact and yet is simple and authentic. Watch this YouTube video: "Unravel Reveal from E3 EA Press Conference 2015."

http://bit.ly/2uOSbmv

The reason I wanted you to see this particular video is that Martin, the speaker, is so genuine, excited, and authentic. Although he is a nervous presenter, it doesn't matter because he connects emotionally with the audience on a deep level. Martin is an excellent example of how being nervous does not have to get in the way of sharing your passion and enthusiasm with listeners. Note also Martin's use of graphics and music in support of his talk.

When I first saw that game trailer, I thought, "Yeah. I want to try that game." And I am not even a gamer! The main point I want to make about this five-minute clip is that about three minutes of it featured Martin's narrative, which prompted people to blog and tweet about it for a full eight months before the game even hit the retail shelves. That's the power of what can happen when you connect emotionally with an audience with a good story.

So I hope that you view stories a little differently now. They are fantastic tools, and people love to hear authentic stories in just about any situation.

29: YOU

The "You" is probably not what you are thinking. When you consider your audience or listener, the "You" in your talk, presentation, demo, or job interview, you will have a much higher chance of connecting emotionally. Why? It's simple. Your listeners need to know that you care about them, whereas most speakers make it mostly about themselves. It's not about you. It's about your audience.

You are the speaker, and of course you are amazing because you have something other people want or need to know. But most people presenting and communicating these days tend to make it all about themselves and not their audience. That's not the way to connect emotionally, and you know it by now or you would not be reading this book. To be persuasive and connect emotionally, whatever you speak about needs to be about your listener and not you.

I have a good friend who is a TED coach named John K. Bates in Salt Lake City, Utah. For over ten years now John has been telling his clients, "Make the audience the hero in your talk, not you." This advice is one of my all-time favorites.

When members of an audience takes things away from your presentation to make their lives better, that's an indication you have successfully connected emotionally with them. Give your listeners reasons why they can take what you've just shared with them and use it in their lives in some way. Make the audience the hero in your talk, and you'll automatically be a hero yourself when they recall something you said or a story you shared.

30: LESS PERFECTION

The last topic I want to talk about that you can use to connect emotionally with your audience is the concept of demanding less perfection from yourself, not more. In business settings, especially when you are communicating and presenting, striving for and achieving some level of perfection can make you seem unapproachable, inaccessible, and unsympathetic. Perfection can backfire. Less perfection will help you get you closer to your authentic self.

I suggest that you strive for excellence instead. You can usually tell when people are excellent communicators or presenters. They seem to care about their listeners, and they show it in the way they address them. Excellence is attainable and repeatable.

People come to me all the time and say, "I want to perfect my presentation or script," to which my first response is, "Then throw it in the garbage!" Typically, you don't need a script except to time your talk to determine whether you can say what you want to say in the time you have been given. Usually this means 18 minutes or less.

You may need a list, outline, or mindmap so that you know what to say when you want to say it. However, memorizing a script is something typically done only by professional actors and actresses. They are trained to remember their lines. More importantly, they know how to get beyond the point of the lines sounding as though they were memorized.

Memorizing a script so that you sound perfect is nonsense because most people are not willing to rehearse to the point where a speech can be presented with authenticity. Please ditch the idea of memorizing your script. Go for authenticity instead. Tell more short stories. Show videos and connect emotionally with your audience by projecting more authenticity, passion, and enthusiasm. When you're successful in that effort, you'll stand out in the minds of your listeners. Perhaps you will even receive a standing ovation after you finish your talk!

So, please, think in terms of less perfection and strive for excellence when speaking. Be authentic and work hard at transferring your enthusiasm for whatever you are talking about to your audience every time you open your mouth. Let your listeners not only "see" the real you but also "feel" the real you. You don't have to fake it. Just be who you are. Get comfortable with being more and more authentic, and you'll find it gets easier to connect emotionally with your audience. Be the friendly and likeable you because likeability is a critical factor in connecting with people.

Speaking of likeability, I love the quotation on the front cover of *The Likeability Factor* by Tim Sanders. It reads, "This book will enrich your life and, more importantly, the lives of those you touch."

Do you realize what this can mean to you and your future listeners? When you increase your likeability, you're expanding the happiness all around you. If you work on your likeability, you may find it easier to connect emotionally with your audience. We can all increase our likeability. It's not that hard.

Finally, according to Ralph Waldo Emerson, "Nothing great was ever achieved without enthusiasm." I agree, especially when you are speaking and communicating.

If you don't transfer your enthusiasm for your topic, product, or service to your audience, you leave it up to them to get enthusiastic after they leave. Do you know how often that happens? Not very often. So it's your job to transfer what you believe to your audience. And it's all conveyed by your authenticity, likeability, and enthusiasm as a speaker.

When you want to transfer your enthusiasm to an audience, it's primarily done through the sound of your voice—how you articulate words, what you emphasize, how you pace your words, how long you pause, and everything else that goes with speaking impactfully. However, know that there is usually a lot more voice in you than just the everyday voice you use when talking to friends or the coffee barista.

The most effective way to improve the way you sound is to seek out a speech or singing coach and ask that person to help you learn what you can do with your voice. Alternatively, search under the word "Improv" in your local area, and you will learn how to be more comfortable with your voice and body in a very safe, fail-free environment. I promise that if you attend an improv meet-up and any type of similar training, it will teach you things about yourself you might never learn on your own.

31: THE LUMINAID STORY

Here is one more story that will illustrate many of the tools and techniques I have covered in this book:

When I was working with the Global Scholars Program at the Ewing Marion Kauffman Foundation in Kansas City, Missouri, I met Anna who was attending Columbia University. She was working on a project when her professor asked the class to help people in need from the devastating 7.0 earthquake in Haiti in 2010. Rather than tell you her story myself, watch Anna share her story, and then I'll update you on what's happened since then.

Watch "LuminAID—Our Story" on this YouTube video:

http://bit.ly/2CYViwY

They were graduate students, by the way. Where are they now in 2019? They had a few struggles because there was a competitor who had a product not unlike their LuminAID. So they went to Indiegogo, ran a fundraising campaign, and exceeded their goal. They raised enough money to make more prototypes and meet more influential people.

Then a few years later they went on *Shark Tank*, season six. Billionaire Mark Cuban invested in their company. Today you can go into just about any sporting-goods store and find their product on the shelves. LuminAID products have gotten bigger and even better. The manufacturer is continually improving the line and growing as a business.

This is an incredible success story with human interest, and I'm guessing that after viewing their video you are connected emotionally to the story too. Don't you want one of these portable lights for yourself and some to give as gifts for emergencies? This was my stocking stuffer one holiday season, and it was the most appreciated item that year. I'm thrilled that the company is still thriving today.

If you watched the LuminAID story, you can skip to the next chapter now. If not, here is a transcript of the video.

"Anna and I started LuminAID because we believe light makes a difference. We were inspired to invent the LuminAID light while we were graduate students in architecture school. It was two weeks after the 2010 earthquake in Haiti.

We were looking at what was being distributed, and we saw that they were distributing medical supplies and shelters and other types of supplies. But there really wasn't a lighting product that was being shipped in volume. And we saw that a lightweight, portable light that was rechargeable could really add a lot of safety and comfort to those victims.

"Typically, after disasters, the lights go out, and the alternatives are something like flashlights, which require batteries. And oftentimes people in certain parts of the world have to use kerosene lanterns or candles, which are dangerous and are fire hazards. Portable solar lighting, like our LuminAID lights, provides a clean and safe alternative to that.

The LuminAID light is a compact solar-rechargeable lantern that packs really small and weighs just a few ounces. There's a solar panel, rechargeable battery, and it inflates to diffuse the light and reduce the glare in your eyes. So if you press the button, it provides over 30 hours of light, and then you just recharge it in the sun. It's totally waterproof and it's made of a really durable and weather-resistant material.

"We sell our lights all over the world, online and in camping centers. Boaters, outdoor recreationists, hikers, campers, they love our lights because they're super lightweight, they're durable, they're easy to charge, compact to carry, and environmentally friendly.

Since that first light, we've grown our company and reached tens of thousands of families across the globe. But we're still just a small group of dedicated people passionate about working together to empower people with light.

"Besides our partnerships with NGOs such as UNFPA, ShelterBox, and Doctors Without Borders, we are also passionate about other ways to give back. So we designed the Give Light Get Light Program, which allows LuminAID supporters to help us make light accessible to all.

Participants receive one LuminAID light for themselves and sponsor a light for a family in need. We've sent more than 20,000 lights to families in more than 50 countries across the globe. We believe that a little light can have a huge impact. LuminAID is proud to help brighten lives around the world."

PART 2: CONCLUSION

I hope that the 18 tools for harnessing your speaking anxiety along with the 10 proven ways to connect emotionally with an audience help you transform yourself into a more amazing, confident, and inspiring speaker. Learning new ways to engage with an audience, such as what has been covered in this book, is a lifelong learning exercise. You can continue to develop your excellence as a speaker for a lifetime.

Take your time learning to use the tools described in Part 1. It takes practice to get comfortable with different types of speaking-anxiety situations. Try to take small steps before you hop on the TED stage with Bill Gates and Warren Buffet sitting in the first row waiting for your talk. Have fun experimenting with the tools described in Part 2 as you learn more about how to connect emotionally with an audience. Keep trying new things until you find the combination that works for you in your specific situation.

I want to be sure to convey one more concept. Try to think of connecting emotionally with your audience as often as possible during your talk using one or more of the proven ways you've read about in this book.

You are free to use any combination of these techniques, just like carpenters use a variety of tools, to make them work in your specific situation. Carefully consider where you might use these techniques in your presentation so that you obtain the maximum effect and emotional response you hope for at points during your talk.

In closing, remember Maya Angelou's statement: "I've learned that people will forget what you said, people will forget what you did, but. . . ." I'll bet you can finish this yourself.

That's right: ". . . they will never forget how you made them feel."

I genuinely hope that this quotation leaves a lasting impression on you as it did on me when I first read it. I also hope that after reading this book you feel as though you have a few techniques that you can take with you and use somehow in your life. My hope is that from now on, when you're meeting, teaching, speaking, communicating, or whatever you're doing, you can more effectively connect emotionally with your audience in ways new to you.

With that, I want to offer you a huge heartfelt thank-you for allowing me the time to share these techniques with you. Now get out there, harness your speaking anxiety, and connect emotionally with your audiences to be more effectively every time you speak. You and your listeners will have a better experience. Perhaps you will even be more inspiring when you speak, by being more authentic, honest, and enthusiastic. Remember, enthusiasm is contagious, and most people like being around enthusiastic people.

I have one final quote for you that has stayed with me ever since I heard it when I was 12 years old. It is something I heard at Camp Turk in Upstate New York at Roundlake from Tom McCord, one of the best storytellers I have ever met. It has always been my favorite quotation, and I hope that you enjoy it too:

Cherish your yesterdays.
Live your todays.
Dream your tomorrows.

WHERE CAN I GET HELP?

Becoming a better speaker, harnessing your speaking anxiety, and delivering a great talk usually require some guidance, perhaps even from a professional. Organizations exist than can help you with speaking anxiety.

Check out Toastmasters International, a worldwide organization that teaches you how to speak in just about any situation. They have clubs in almost every city in the world. Most have weekly meetings for about an hour before work starts the next morning. You get to hang out with people who also are working on their presentation skills. You learn more tools, tips, and techniques to practice in projecting an authentic persona. Toastmasters International also helps you to get rid of linguistic disfluencies in your speech patterns. What's that you say? It's those filler non-words such as "um," "em," "uh," "like," "so," "okay," etc.

If you like this organization or one of its chapters, you can join for very little money. If you get hooked, think about entering some of the speaking competitions in your chapter. Then you can go even further since it is a worldwide organization. You can compete in a country, geographical region, and even the world at large. Toastmasters sponsors a championship event that attracts people from all over the world. Winning these types of competitions enhances a speaker's career. I've seen some go on to earn as much as $100,000 USD for a one-hour talk.

On this same note, if you want to improve your speaking ability, I suggest that you take several improv classes. They will quickly help you to get more comfortable with your voice and body, part of the key to becoming an accomplished speaker. Improvisation clubs can be found on sites such as Meetup.com and Eventbrite.com. The first class will teach you things about yourself you never knew, and you will do things you never thought possible. Those experiences will automatically help you to harness your speaking anxiety.

Here's a response I heard from an improv meet-up leader who posed the question, "Why would you use improv to help with public speaking?" Her response was as follows: "Well, the real objective of improv is, 'How can we get you to reduce your self-consciousnesses around your voice and your body?' When you get your body on your side, you start acting like a confident person. The good news for new people coming to an improv class is that it is not only for actors and actresses, and there are no improv police. You cannot fail at this."

It's as simple as that. You can't fail at improv, and it can be life-altering in a very positive way. If you go to one or more classes, you will be a changed person. People will notice how much more confident you have become. You will learn things you can do with your voice and body that you never thought possible.

LET'S CONNECT

I am a big believer in connecting with my readers through LinkedIn or any other method you prefer.

Here is my eBusiness Card:

https://mingl.no/nathan

ABOUT THE AUTHOR

 Nathan Gold is the Chief Coach of The Demo Coach. He hails from the San Francisco Bay Area and travels the world speaking about and coaching people on how to prepare for high-stakes speaking opportunities and how to harness their speaking anxiety. Nathan does this through keynotes, interactive workshops, live streaming, and 1:1 sessions, both in person and online.

He has personally delivered thousands of presentations along with thousands of hours of professional coaching while working with companies such as, SanDisk, IBM, Kaiser Permanente, Glue Networks, Bill.com, Education.com, GetAround.com, Innovation Norway,—on designing, scripting and delivering more compelling and memorable presentations and product demos, especially in situations where you cannot afford to miss.

Nathan was born in the late 1950s. Growing up, his favorite show was Star Trek where he was mesmerized by the spaceships, phasers, tricorders, universal translators, and especially, the communicators. That program started his love for technology.

In high school, he excelled at computers. After finishing a 14-week programming course in the first three weeks of class, his teachers were so impressed they sent him upstairs to work with the school's IBM 1130 mainframe, the first of its kind in any High School on Long Island. That is where Nathan began teaching computer programming in the adult education program at the age of 16. He worked with students three times his age and loved the interaction with adults, especially when holding the chalk.

Nathan went on to the SUNY Maritime College in Throggs Neck, New York thinking he would enter maritime work and sail the ocean while seeing ports all around the world. After one year, he realized spending 6-months at sea was not going to work for him. He went on to spend the next three years at SUNY Stony Brook, where Nathan majored in Computer Science. While there, the Computer Science Department made him a teaching assistant and he helped students with all sorts of computer software and hardware issues.

Right out of college, he designed and delivered mainframe computer programming classes at National Westminster Bank on Long Island. However, Nathan had a dream to live by the beach in California and travel the world while working for a high-tech company. That dream was not coming true on Long Island.

On Labor Day 1980, Nathan packed everything he owned into his beat-up Oldsmobile and headed for California, even though he had never been there before. Within five days of arriving, Nathan had four job interviews in Los Angeles and three in San Diego. He ended up choosing a small software company with about 30 people in San Diego named ISSCO Graphics, where he spent seven years traveling around the world training their customers how to use mainframe computer graphics software. At ISSCO and throughout his career, Nathan was the one go-to guy for all high-level executive sales briefings, trade shows, press issues, and analysts' product demo needs because he was able to take complex topics and make them enjoyable for any audience.

In early 1990, Nathan fell in love with pen computers and mobile computing. He spent over 10 years working with people all over the world, evangelizing technology such as the PenPoint operating system and the original Palm Pilot. During this time, he started helping other people with their product demos as a favor because he really enjoys helping people achieve more success in life.

After his time at Extensity in the early 2000s demonstrating the first enterprise class Java application Sun had ever seen delivered, Nathan went back to college to finish the degree he started in 1975. After roughly one year attending university as the oldest person in every class, Nathan finally received his BA Multidisciplinary Degree from SUNY Stony Brook in 2002 with emphasis in Computer Science, Mathematics, and Theatre.

In April 2008, Nathan started The Demo Coach business because he believed he could help other people learn to deliver more compelling, memorable, and captivating presentations. He currently specializes in helping people harness their speaking anxiety and use that newfound energy, authenticity and enthusiasm to connect emotionally to the audience. Throughout the last decade, Nathan has coached thousands of people around the world for high stakes speaking opportunities in TED talks, keynotes, sales meetings, trade shows, investor pitches, and even job interviews.

Nathan is a two-time winner of the distinguished DEMOgod Award, given to him at DEMOmobile 2000 for being "A one-man walking communications store with the ability to deliver an incredibly well-timed demonstration." At DEMOfall 2005, for his demo of U3 he was presented with his second DEMgod Award. He is also the co-author of Giving Memorable Product Demos, available on Amazon.com.

The Wall Street Journal called Nathan an "elevator pitch expert" after coaching the Top 5 Finalists in the Startup of the Year award, in the actual WSJ elevators in NYC. He's the pitch coach for dozens of accelerators and incubators around the world, an Industry Fellow at UC Berkeley and Hong Kong Baptist University, and a guest lecturer at Wharton Entrepreneurship. Nathan is featured on The Kauffman Founders School website in a video series called Powerful Presentations and Mastering Q&A.

KEYNOTES AND WORKSHOPS

As an internationally recognized speaker, coach, and trainer, I deliver over 150 keynote talks per year on presentation, communication, and networking skills. I edutain audiences of all sizes in as little as 15-minutes or as long as 3 hours. All keynote talks are designed to empower people who speak in high-stakes situations such as a TED talk, investor pitches, keynotes, board meetings, peer meetings, job interviews and those do-or-die can't miss sales calls.

These keynote talks are full of "solid nourishment" and no "empty calories". Each topic below is designed to be flexible to accommodate various types of audiences including both business and entrepreneurs and comes with an optional Brainstorming Exercise.

Words people frequently use to describe
Keynotes and Workshops by Nathan:

Inspiring, Fun, Motivating, Thought-provoking

Keynote and Workshop descriptions:

1. **How to Harness Your Speaking Anxiety**
   Everyone has speaking anxiety. Some people use it as a powerful tool while others let it stop them cold in their tracks from even speaking up. This keynote is designed to help you harness your speaker anxiety and turn it into a powerful

tool you can use during formal presentations, weekly staff meetings, or even during job interviews. You will hear about proven tools, techniques, and tips, many backed by science and research, that you can start using immediately to harness your speaking anxiety.

2. **Proven Ways to Connect Emotionally with Your Audience**
People always say the best presenters have a knack for getting you to feel something. They usually do this by creating a situation where their audience responds with one or more emotions. In some talks, you experience these multiple times. This talk will share 10 proven ways you can do this with your audience of 1 or many. It's actually very simple once you discover how persuasive people have been doing this since language was invented. Using the tools, tips, and techniques demonstrated in this talk, you will be able to generate your own authentic emotional response from people in your next presentation or in a conversation with anyone.

3. **How to Captivate Any Audience in Less Than 30-Seconds**
In this talk, attendees will hear about The Red Box Method, which includes nine tools to help presenters captivate their audience more quickly, easily, and dramatically. The audience will learn techniques on how to be more memorable in any high-stakes presenting situation such as with a TED talk, keynote, board meeting, investor pitch, sales meeting, or job interview. After this talk, attendees will be better prepared to present more confidently, close more deals, persuade more investors, and you may even receive a standing ovation.

4. **AHA! Networking 2.0**
Networking is a bit of both art and science. This talk will help anyone who has hesitation or difficulty connecting or

generating a conversation with someone new. It will help alleviate the anxiety of those initial few minutes because you will be armed with tools to help in any networking situation. Attendees will learn how to instantly find something in common with anyone anywhere on the planet, how to become the most sought-after person in the room, and how to start creating more meaningful, lasting relationships. This talk will energize the crowd and especially helpful to any audience after a long day of conferencing just before breaking for drinks, networking, and dinner.

5. **Q&A: Mastering the Unpredictable**

Handling question-and-answer sessions before, during, or after a presentation is a continuation of the presentation but is often overlooked. This talk will teach attendees how to be more effective and confident when facing those unpredictable situations with an audience. The techniques shared here will ultimately give presenters tools to be more confident, competent, and authentic in how they answer any question, including the ones to which the answer is not known.

6. **Designing an Unforgettable Handshake Introduction**

When people greet each other for the first time, often they ask, "What does your company do?" This talk will prepare attendees for this most common question received in business. Using the Handshake Introduction framework, everyone will be prepared to offer a compelling answer whether talking to one person, participating on a panel in front of hundreds of people, or facing the interview question "Tell me about yourself." Using the techniques shared in this talk, attendees will be more effective at standing out in a crowd.

7. **How to Design and Deliver a TEDx-like Talk**

   TED talks are famous for how their presenters deliver stories, insights, and extraordinary information in 18-minutes or less. This talk extrapolates the main techniques people use on the TED stages to captivate audiences from all around the world. Attendees can start using what they learn in their next presentation, such as how to make the audience the hero in their talks, not the presenters themselves.

8. **Persuade Anyone with Five Slides in Five Minutes**

   This talk unveils a simple, effective, and proven framework for persuading an audience with five slides in 5-minutes or less. Attendees will learn how to synthesize their message into one sentence to compel their audiences to pay very close attention to their pitch. The techniques discussed in this talk are constantly in use by some of the most confident, competent, and memorable presenters. Attendees will be able to use this framework in their next presentation.

9. **Avoiding the Top 12 Mistakes People Make When Presenting**

   People make dozens of mistakes when presenting, but all those mistakes can be avoided. This talk will make visible the top 12 mistakes people make when presenting and address how to avoid them. It includes giving too much information on one slide to avoiding boring, sleepy, and ineffective slideware. Attendees will also hear about forcing the audience to read their slides, not using enough visuals, and not connecting with the audience on an emotional level.

10. **Custom Keynote or Workshop**

    If you have a specific keynote or workshop related to these topics you want delivered, Nathan will customize the time he spends with your audience to be sure their time and learnings are maximized.

One of the main benefits of these workshops is the results people get from the Brainstorming Exercises. The results always seem to surprise participants with how much they can accomplish within a very short time frame. Depending on the goals of the people attending, workshop length can range from 18-minutes to 2-days. All of these workshops can be delivered in person or online. For more details, please contact me.